Red Factor Canary

Other titles of interest:

A BIRDKEEPER'S GUIDE TO

PET BIRDS

Yellow Masked Lovebirds

Grey Parrot taking food from hand

A BIRDKEEPER'S GUIDE TO

PET BIRDS

A practical introduction to maintaining and enjoying a wide range of pet birds in the home

David Alderton

No. 16081

A Salamander Book

Fawn Zebra Finch

Credits

Editor: Geoff Rogers   Design: Graeme Campbell
Colour reproductions:
Melbourne Graphics Ltd.
Filmset: SX Composing Ltd.
Printed in Portugal

Author

David Alderton has kept and bred a wide variety of birds for over twenty years. He has travelled extensively in pursuit of this interest, visiting other enthusiasts in various parts of the world, including the United States, Canada and Australia. He has previously written a number of books on avicultural subjects, and contributes regularly to general and specialist publications in the UK and overseas. David studied veterinary medicine at Cambridge University, and now, in addition to writing, runs a highly respected international service that offers advice on the needs of animals kept in both domestic and commercial environments. He is also a Council Member of the Avicultural Society.

Photographer

Cyril Laubscher has been interested in aviculture and ornithology for more than thirty years and has travelled extensively in Europe, Australia and Southern Africa photographing wildlife. When he left England for Australia in 1966 as an enthusiastic aviculturalist, this fascination found expression as he began to portray birds photographically. In Australia he met the well-known aviculturalist Stan Sindel and, as a result of this association, seventeen of Cyril's photographs were published in Joseph Forshaw's original book on Australian Parrots in 1969. Since then, his photographs have met with considerable acclaim and the majority of those that appear here were taken specially for this book.

Contents

Introduction

Keeping birds as pets is a traditional pastime that dates back thousands of years, and now appears to be enjoying an upsurge in popularity. There are various social reasons for this growth in interest. In the first instance, owning a pet bird in an urban environment does not create the potential difficulties associated with keeping a dog or cat in such surroundings. Furthermore, as households become smaller and more people live on their own, attitudes towards companion animals are changing. It is no coincidence that members of the parrot family, including the Budgerigar, are most highly valued by the petseeker. This is undoubtedly because these birds can become true companions. They have tractable natures, and can mimic the human voice and other sounds with startling accuracy. This particular characteristic is an important factor in the choice of a pet, especially for people living alone.

Studies carried out in different countries have revealed the

benefits of pet bird ownership for people of all ages. Elderly people in particular appreciate owning a pet that is easy to look after and which provides a responsive companion in their lives. Contact with a tame bird also has a beneficial effect on health for every age group, reducing stress and in many cases leading to a detectable fall in blood pressure. Indeed, keeping a bird as a pet offers a means of true relaxation, both mental and physical, in an increasingly stressful world.

While social trends favour more widespread keeping of pet birds, breeders of parrots are also contributing to the rising interest in this area. Now that the reproductive requirements of such birds are becoming much better understood, it is possible to hand rear chicks from the egg. Baby parrots used to human company from the start will develop into marvellously tame pets, and will tend to display their powers of mimicry from an early age.

Which birds make the best pets?

For many people, the Budgerigar is the obvious choice as a pet bird. Millions of these delightful parakeets are kept as companions throughout the world. They are readily obtainable and easy to cater for, both in terms of their housing and feeding needs. They will learn to talk quite readily – especially if obtained when young – and have an attractive natural chattering call.

Set against these ideal qualities in a pet bird, how do other choices compare? Here, we briefly review the rewards and possible difficulties associated with keeping various types of birds as pets.

Large parrots

Large parrots are both much more costly to acquire and considerably more demanding than their small relatives, such as the Budgerigar. Parrots are likely to become extremely devoted to their owners, however, and should live for decades. A pet parrot can become a lifetime companion. Nevertheless, they have some drawbacks which you need to consider before obtaining one of these fine birds.

Above: *The tame and lively nature of the Budgerigar is clearly shown here. Budgies make great companions for people of all ages.*

They have large and powerful beaks which can wreak devastation on furniture. This also means that they need careful handling, especially if they are not tame, when they may bite if any attempt is made to restrain them. Routine handling is rarely required though, unless the bird is ill or refuses to return to its cage after being allowed out into a room for exercise.

Because of their destructive capabilities, housing parrots satisfactorily is an expensive undertaking. In addition, although many species are valued as talented mimics, they also have loud and

Below: *Recent studies have shown that companion birds lower stress in their owners more than any other pet. Parrots, such as this cockatoo, will become tame and learn to mimic, if obtained young.*

raucous natural calls, which can cause problems within the domestic environment, especially to close neighbours. Even hand-reared birds do not lose this trait, although it is possible to restrict periods of such noise by careful training, as described on pages 45-47.

Those species of parrot which normally form relatively strong pair bonds are most suitable as pets, since they do not resent close contact with their owners. Indeed, they will actively seek to have the side of the head tickled in imitation of the preening actions of a mate.

Difficulties can arise, however, once a bird becomes sexually mature, usually in terms of a change in temperament. This tends to happen with pairs of parrots housed in aviaries. Cock cockatoos, for example, may become very aggressive towards their intended mates, and can even kill a prospective partner that shows insufficient inclination to nest. Similarly, a tame bird may resort to biting its owner unexpectedly, and so caution is advisable, especially with mature cock cockatoos.

Below: *The Cockatiel has much in its favour as a pet bird. It is freely available in a wide range of colours, inexpensive and has a quiet voice, unlike many parrots. An ideal pet for children.*

Cockatiels and lovebirds

For a home with children, the delightful Cockatiel is probably more suitable, since it shows none of the temperamental weaknesses of its close relatives in the parrot family. Indeed, the Cockatiel is rapidly gaining in popularity, and can now be acquired in a wide range of colours. These birds closely resemble cockatoos in appearance, but are easily distinguishable by their long tails. Cockatiels can become good mimics, and cocks especially have a pleasant song.

The Peach-faced Lovebird is another species that has been bred in a host of colour forms during recent years. Although generally viewed as an aviary bird, they can make suitable pets for the home and are very popular in Australia for this reason. Again, hand-reared individuals tend to settle best in domestic surroundings, but recently fledged youngsters can also become tame.

Other popular pet birds

Of course, it is not only members of the parrot family that are able to mimic human speech. Other species share this characteristic, most notably the Greater Hill Mynah, which is a member of the starling family. The clear intonation of these mynah birds is unsurpassed, but although they can

become tame – often feeding from the hand – they do not relish the close contact which forms part of the appeal of keeping one of the larger parrots. Another point to bear in mind before deciding on these birds is that they need a diet based on fruit and other soft foods and, as a result, they can prove messy, especially in the confines of a relatively small cage.

Some birds are highly valued as pets although they neither talk nor become exceptionally tame. The domesticated Canary – a member of the finch family – is a supreme example of a pet bird which has maintained its popularity amongst petseekers for centuries, essentially because of its attractive song. Since it is the cock birds that are most favoured for their song, canaries are usually obtained several months after fledging, when the cocks may be distinguished by their song. Various breeds of canary are well established, and are available in a wide range of colours and markings.

Certain finches are especially popular with children, since they are easy to keep and will usually nest readily and successfully in cage surroundings. Both the Zebra Finch and the Bengalese, or Society Finch, are ideal in these respects, although neither species is a talented songster. Indeed, the rather plaintive and monotonous

Above: *Red Factor Canary. Apart from the traditional canary yellow forms, these popular songsters can be obtained in other colours.*

calls of the Zebra Finch can become disturbing if heard for too long at close quarters. However, Zebra Finches are more likely to breed successfully because they are easy to sex, certainly in comparison with Bengalese Finches.

Although finches are in no way destructive, and therefore can be housed without difficulty, they are very quick when in flight and difficult

Below: *A pair of Zebra Finches, with the hen on the left. These birds nest readily in the home, but will not become very tame.*

Hen (Female)

Cock (Male)

to catch if they are loose in a room.
This can make them unsuitable for
handicapped or infirm owners. In
contrast, budgerigars and parrots
generally return to their quarters
quite readily when they are let out
into the room.

A bird in the home
Irrespective of species, a pet bird in
the home will inevitably cause some
degree of mess. It is possible to
minimize the spread of seed husks,
for example, but additional cleaning
will inevitably be required. Be sure to
consider this before obtaining a
bird; it can be a strong deterrent for

Above: *Golden Cherry Peach-
faced Lovebird. One of many
colour forms now available. Not
difficult to handle or care for.*

some potential owners. In addition,
feather dust may prove a direct
source of discomfort to a few
people, typically causing a tight-
chested feeling. This is more
commonly encountered in the
company of cockatoos than with
other birds. Spraying the bird
regularly and wiping around the
immediate vicinity of the cage with a
damp cloth to remove dust will help
to prevent this problem arising.

How ionizers work

Negative voltage applied to needle

Negative ions spread into room

High-energy electrons produce negative ions

Dust particle

Earthed surface

Installing an ionizer in the room can also help to reduce the level of dust in the air. These electrical devices produce a harmless stream of negative ions that cause airborne particles to settle out.

Another source of worry can be the havoc a bird might cause once it is loose in a room. Parrots can certainly inflict considerable damage on woodwork, including furniture, and so it is important to supervise these birds once they are let out of their quarters. Keeping an eye on the bird also makes it easy for you to clear up fresh droppings with a piece of cotton-wool or damp tissue, so that no trace is left behind. Alternatively, you can build a large indoor flight for your bird, so reducing the need to let the bird out so regularly. This is ideal for finches, since it is unwise to allow them out of their quarters because of the difficulty of catching them again.

Unless it is kept with a suitable companion, regular human contact is vital for the well-being of a pet parrot. Parrots are generally gregarious creatures by nature and they will pine if they are kept alone with little attention from their owner. In this respect, they can be just as demanding as a dog. The behavioural difficulties encountered in some parrots can be traced back to neglect of this type; feather plucking can arise in this way, for example (see pages 19 and 56).

If you feel that you are unable to devote sufficient time to a pet parrot, consider obtaining a pair of finches or even a canary, which are far less dependent on maintaining a close relationship with their owner.

Above: *If you have an ionizer in the room alongside your bird, this will help to keep the environment clean. Feather dust can be a problem with certain birds such as cockatoos. An ionizer produces a stream of electrons from its tip, which form negative ions that combine with dust particles and precipitate them from the air.*

Birds with other pets

It can be difficult to keep a bird safely in a household where a number of cats are already present. Even if a cat cannot reach the bird directly through the mesh of the cage, it can still cause the bird considerable distress, and may actually knock the cage over, injuring the bird in the process. It seems that small finches are most likely to attract a cat's attention, but all birds are potentially at risk. Conversely, if a parrot retaliates against the cat, then this also could cause injury. Some cats are worse than others in the company of birds, but no cat can be entirely trusted in this regard.

Dogs usually accept the addition of a pet bird to the home without showing any concern. On occasions, parrots can become jealous of dogs, however, and may screech repeatedly if they see the dog apparently usurping their place in their owner's affection.

A similar problem may arise when introducing a new bird alongside an established pet bird, even if they are known to be of the opposite sex. This applies notably to the larger parrots, such as macaws, especially if the established pet has been kept on its own for a long period. Introducing a new bird is not simply a matter of placing one bird in the cage with the other; severe fighting will almost certainly break out. The birds must be introduced gradually. This means housing them close together in separate cages. Each should then come to accept the presence of its neighbour. Never position the cages so that the birds can reach each other through the bars, however, since each bird may injure the feet of its potential companion or even the tongue, which is likely to bleed profusely.

Breeding parrots in the home

Providing that they are not rushed, parrots will usually accept each other without subsequent problems, but the introductory phase may well take several months. Even large parrots, such as the multicoloured macaws, may be bred successfully in the home. The birds are likely to lose interest in their owner, however, and may well become aggressive to intrusions during this phase. They will need a stout nestbox attached to their quarters. This should feature an inspection panel through which you can monitor the development of the chicks at critical stages.

Breeding parrots provides an additional fascinating insight into the habits of these birds. Although the adult pair are unlikely to be as tame as they may have been before being introduced to each other, you can hope for the compensation of at least one chick, which should itself develop into a marvellous companion. If you start with an older parrot which shows little sign of becoming truly tame, then breeding may well be an option worth considering to redress the balance.

Below: *Larger parrots, such as this Mealy Amazon, can undergo a change in temperament, becoming aggressive in breeding condition.*

Choosing a healthy bird

You can obtain pet birds from various sources, and it will repay you to study the options carefully, especially if you are seeking a larger parrot. These birds are costly, and prices can vary considerably. What appears to be a bargain may not necessarily prove to make the best pet in the long term. Hand-reared parrots invariably command the highest price, because of the huge input of time necessary to raise chicks successfully from the egg by artificial means. The advantage of such birds is that they will have no fear of humans, and should settle readily in the domestic environment.

It is not difficult to contact breeders of parrots. Depending on the species required, you may be able to obtain a genuine youngster locally. Their addresses can be found in the advertisement columns of the many avicultural magazines that are produced around the world. This applies especially to cockatiels and budgerigars, and indeed these may be advertised in local newspapers.

Trade suppliers
Pet stores often stock a variety of species, but their selection of parrots tends to be rather limited. Furthermore, they often stock imported birds, which may prove more difficult to establish than hand-reared chicks. A controlled trade in wild-caught parrots provides a means of managing their numbers in areas where they inflict damage on crops. By this means, parrots are tolerated by the native people for their commercial value; otherwise they could be persecuted.

Exporting countries typically impose a levy on their birds, so that trade can fund other conservation programmes and research. The transfer of birds from country to country is restricted, however, by conservation controls arising from the internationally accepted Convention on International Trade in Endangered Species of Wild Fauna and Flora (CITES) and, in most cases, by quarantine restrictions. This applies to the

Below: *Do not rush into buying a pet bird. Remember that you will be obtaining a companion to share your life for perhaps ten years or more. For a tame, talking bird you should obtain a genuine youngster.*

movement of pet birds as well as to commercial shipments. Advice on importing can usually be obtained from the appropriate agricultural department. They will advise you on quarantine regulations, on what other documentation you may require and where to obtain this.

Parrot farms

Breeding farms for parrots are becoming increasingly common and offer perhaps the widest choice of young stock. They also advertise in the avicultural magazines and, even if they are not in your locality, it is well worth visiting them before deciding upon any particular bird on offer. Do not feel pressured to buy a parrot unless you are entirely happy with your choice, especially since ownership will prove to be a long-term commitment.

Plumage as a health guide

The condition of a bird's feathering is an important guide to its overall state of health, especially in members of the parrot family. These birds normally have a sleek appearance at close quarters. A sick bird usually has ruffled plumage and appears relatively dull and uninterested. The plumage of recently imported stock may be relatively scruffy but this is not necessarily a serious problem, since their plumage will be replaced at the next moult. Here, we review possible plumage problems and how to recognize them.

Feather plucking The larger parrots are prone to the vice of feather plucking, however, and this can be a very difficult problem to overcome once it has become established. Distinctive signs include the presence of greyish, downy plumage, typically on the chest. In more severe cases, bald areas are apparent. Some species seem more susceptible to this vice than others, with grey parrots, macaws and cockatoos most likely to be affected.

A young bird with a relatively sparse covering of feathers, typically at the back of the neck, is

likely to have been plucked by its parents while still in the nest. Budgerigars and Lutino cockatiels are the birds most commonly affected. The plumage may, in fact, be regrowing by the time that the young birds are feeding themselves. The new feathers will appear as spikes protruding through the skin. As during a normal moult, the protective waxy casing breaks down, largely through the bird's preening, and the plumage unfurls.

Feather plucking of this type is of no real significance to the pet owner. It can be an inherited trait, however, and birds plucked by their parents may well pluck their own offspring. Significantly, however, birds which have been plucked in the nest are no more likely to pluck themselves later if life than other birds. But in a few cases, particularly with Lutino cockatiels, plucked chicks can prove more nervous, so that it is advisable to seek a perfectly feathered youngster at the outset.

Feather rot Another, more serious disorder which can be confused with feather plucking is the disease known as feather rot, which at present seems to affect only cockatoos. The early signs are similar, but in feather rot the whole body is affected, including areas which a bird living on its own is unable to pluck, such as the sides of its head. The plumage is frail, and although new feathers emerge these are lost before they have

Below: *Check the plumage of cockatoos carefully. They can be afflicted with the viral disease feather rot, as shown here.*

developed to any extent. Since there is no effective treatment for this progressive and ultimately fatal disorder, you should look very carefully before acquiring a cockatoo that shows clear signs of any plumage disorder.

French moult A weakness, widely recognized in young budgerigars and occasionally found in lovebirds and cockatiels, is known as French moult. Affected birds lose their tail and flight feathers to a variable extent soon after they leave the nest. This will clearly handicap their powers of flight, although in some cases the birds recover spontaneously. The disease has very localized effects, and the plumage covering the body is usually unaffected.

Feather lice The presence of parasites may be another cause of feather plucking. Feather lice are not generally a major problem, but they can cause noticeable feather damage. This is most likely to affect the plumage on the breast, back and over the wings. The individual feathers, instead of having a smooth outline, appear to have chewed edges. Although such damage cannot be repaired until the feathers are shed during the next moult, the parasites themselves are easy to eradicate using a special aerosol preparation.

Making a closer examination
Before making a decision, watch the bird quietly for a few minutes. Healthy birds will preen themselves, although excessively frenetic preening coupled with poor plumage condition often indicates the presence of external parasites. Many birds will rest with just one leg on the perch. This is quite normal and need not be a cause for concern, unless the bird avoids using its other leg once it starts to move around its quarters.

It is often easier to carry out a close examination of a bird by catching it, but before you do this, take the opportunity to check its respiration. Indeed, it may not be

Above: *Budgerigars suffering from French moult may be unable to fly properly, since their flight and tail feathers are often lost.*

possible to gain a reliable indication of the bird's breathing after handling it, since this tends to lead to a rapid increase in the respiratory rate. Listening close to the cage may enable you to detect any wheezing, although watching the slight tail movements which occur as the bird breathes can be a more reliable guide. If these movements seem laboured, the bird might well be afflicted with a breathing ailment.

Breathing ailments
It may be that the bird is suffering from the fungal disease known as aspergillosis. A chronic ailment, aspergillosis is difficult to treat at best, and the infection may not be diagnosed until the disease is well advanced. While any bird species may be affected, aspergillosis is most often seen in the *Pionus* parrots. These, unfortunately, show a tendency to wheeze if they are frightened, and this can make diagnosis difficult. In most cases, parrots with aspergillosis tend to be slightly lethargic, and may also have difficulty in flying.

Another potential cause of breathing distress is a blockage of the nostrils. This can be the result of an infection or, in the case of young birds, a plug of the rearing mixture becoming hardened over the top of the beak. It is always worth checking the nostrils in any case, even if there is no apparent problem.

A long-standing minor infection can lead to one of the openings of the nostrils becoming larger than the other. This may not prove significant, but if the bird is still carrying the infection, this could flare up when it is moved to a new environment. The symptoms may be relatively minor, such as a persistent discharge from one nostril, but there is no guarantee

Below: *The preening behaviour shown by this Tucuman Amazon is a sign that the bird is in good health. Sick birds rarely attempt to preen and look dull and listless.*

that this will not develop into a more generalized infection. Conversely, if a parrot sneezes, this may not necessarily indicate any ailment. It could simply be that dust has irritated the nasal passages. An accompanying discharge, however, is a more serious matter. Look also for any signs of swelling around the eyes, or matting of the feathers in this area. This could indicate a nasal infection, especially if the bird is reluctant to open its eyes.

The bird in the hand
Ask the vendor to catch the bird of your choice, so that you can check it carefully at closer quarters. With budgerigars in particular, deviations of the beak are not uncommon. In the case of young birds, look closely to see if the upper beak curls inside the lower part. Budgerigars with this

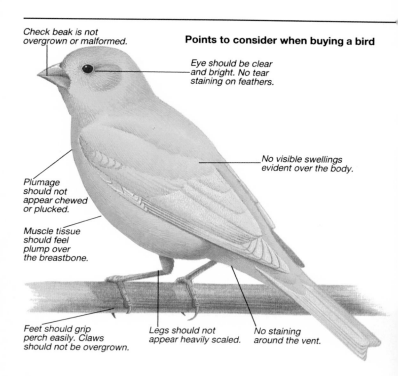

Check beak is not overgrown or malformed.

Points to consider when buying a bird

Eye should be clear and bright. No tear staining on feathers.

No visible swellings evident over the body.

Plumage should not appear chewed or plucked.

Muscle tissue should feel plump over the breastbone.

Feet should grip perch easily. Claws should not be overgrown.

Legs should not appear heavily scaled.

No staining around the vent.

Above: *Looking at the bird quietly can reveal much about its state of health. This diagram shows the main points to look for; more specific considerations may also apply, depending on the bird.*

defect will need to have their beaks trimmed regularly throughout their lives if they are to continue eating without difficulty (see page 55).

Also check the beak for evidence of scaly face mites. These mites burrow into the tissue, creating coral-like encrustations over a period of time. It is unlikely that the signs of scaly face will be apparent in a recently fledged budgerigar, but be sure to check older individuals carefully (see page 59). Treatment is straightforward if begun early, but permanent disfigurement of the beak will result once the disease is well advanced, so avoid badly affected individuals.

One of the most reliable indicators of a bird's overall state of health is the covering of muscle tissue around the breastbone. The breastbone can be felt as a bony prominence running down the middle of the breast. A bird which is sick or undernourished will show a clear hollow on either side of the breastbone, and such loss of muscle tissue is usually described as 'going light'. It is commonly associated with long-term illnesses such as aspergillosis, although a sudden digestive upset will also lead to weight loss of this type.

Conversely, if the edge of the breastbone is hardly discernible then the bird is obese. Pet birds kept in cages tend to suffer more from this problem than their aviary counterparts, because they usually have less opportunity to exercise. This may in turn affect their ability to fly, although less obvious internal problems brought on by obesity, such as fatty deposits in the liver and elsewhere in the body, are more likely to curtail the bird's lifespan.

Always check that established pet birds show no signs of external swellings, which could be further evidence of obesity. Budgerigars, for example, are prone to swellings called lipomas, which occur typically on or close to the breastbone. These benign fatty tumours also restrict the bird's flying power. Although surgery may be possible to remove them, recurrences are not uncommon. (See also page 57.)

Why a young bird?
It is certainly preferable to obtain a genuine young bird in the first instance, since such a bird will not have acquired any vices. Some parrots can be selective in their acceptance of an owner, developing a dislike of men, for example, and this can create difficulties in the home. In addition it is usually harder to teach adult parrots to expand their vocabularies, especially if they have been used to another owner.

While it is not unusual for parrots to form a strong bond with one member of the family, it will be easier to integrate a young bird fully into family life. In any case, do not be surprised if an adult tame parrot proves withdrawn during its early days in a new home; some individuals settle quicker than others. Never attempt to force the

Below: *Always check the eyes in the case of a young parrot. The iris around the pupil is typically dark, as in this baby Orange-winged Amazon. A young bird should settle in quickly and tame more easily than a mature bird. Hand-reared parrots are a case in point.*

bird into accepting your attentions; proceed patiently.

Mynah birds are by nature less sensitive than most parrots, and so are less likely to be disturbed by a change in their surroundings. Indeed, they will probably not show any adverse reaction to a move. The main drawback of buying an adult talking mynah bird is that its age will almost certainly be unknown. Furthermore an adult will cost relatively more than a youngster and there is no guarantee that the bird will be tame. Since the potential lifespan of a mynah bird is relatively short compared with that of most parrots – few live for longer than fifteen years or so – a young bird (known as a 'gaper') should prove the best investment.

Buying finches
One of the best indicators of health in a finch is its level of activity. Both Bengalese and Zebra finches are lively birds by nature, spending much of their time hopping and flying around their quarters. Some Zebra finches, in particular, can appear scruffy, but this need not be a cause for undue concern. If kept short of nesting material, or in overcrowded conditions, these finches will resort to plucking feathers from their companions. However, this does not prove to be a persistent vice as is usually the case with parrots. If their environmental conditions are improved, the plumage of these small birds will regrow in due course. Avoid finches which appear fluffed up and inactive, especially if they show any soiling of the plumage around the vent. This usually indicates a digestive tract disorder, which could prove contagious.

If you follow the general points raised in this section in conjunction with the specific details about each particular species in the second part of the book, you should be assured of obtaining a bird that will develop into a lively companion. Before you actually take this step, however, you should consider what type of accommodation to provide for your particular choice of bird.

Housing your pet bird

It is surprising just how many different types of cages are available. Do not be misled into choosing an expensive and ornate design, without actually examining the cage for its primary purpose. Far too many cages presently being marketed are not suitable, in various significant respects, for housing birds. In the first instance, the cage should be as large as possible, especially if the bird is going to be confined for much of the day. The ornate designs generally have a totally inadequate flight area, and circular cages offer no real flying space. Finches in particular suffer from being housed in circular cages, which force them to fly in a totally artificial manner and also offer these rather nervous birds very little cover.

Parrot cages

Cages for parrots need to be robust and constructed in such a way that they will not injure any occupant. Unfortunately, economies in manufacture have led to an increasing number of injuries caused by basic flaws in cage design. These are especially apparent around the base of the cage. The usual parrot cage consists of a top mesh unit attached to a lower metal base. This base can have sharp edges which may cut the bird's claw or toe. Parrots are especially at risk in this regard, because they spend much of their time climbing around their cage. Any clear joins in the sheet metal can prove equally dangerous, and may trap and even amputate a parrot's toe.

Various coverings are used on the upper mesh part of bird cages. Check that galvanized bars have no sharp edges; the splinters can be very sharp, and may penetrate a parrot's tongue and cause profuse bleeding. If a sharp fragment is swallowed it could lodge lower down in the digestive tract and cause serious complications.

Also check the cage fittings supplied and change them as necessary. Plastic food containers, for example, while suitable for smaller members of the parrot

Above: *Parrots are intelligent birds, and may soon learn to escape from their cage, sometimes when there is no one at home. This can be dangerous, and may also lead to damage, such as chewed furniture. A padlock on the cage door can be a good investment.*

family, such as budgerigars and even cockatiels, will be easily destroyed by larger parrots with more powerful beaks. Plastic is fairly brittle and can be broken into sharp fragments. Among the alternatives are galvanized metal or ceramic pots. The latter are preferable, since they will not react with any chemicals, such as a tonic, administered in drinking water.

Door fastenings on parrot cages are another area where basic design faults often appear. A simple hook is totally inadequate. Even doors closed by means of a nut tightened in place are not entirely safe. Some parrots can learn to undo this nut —

possibly through watching their owner – by using the vice-like grip of their beaks to twist the nut loose. Clearly, it can be dangerous as well as damaging if a parrot escapes into the room when no one is present. To be sure, use a chain and a padlock to secure the door.

Housing mynahs

Special cages are marketed for mynah birds, usually of a box-type design which helps to contain the droppings of these birds. Unfortunately, these cages are invariably too small. Since few people like to allow mynahs loose into a room, because of their messy habits, it is vital to accommodate these active birds permanently in spacious surroundings.

The ideal size for a mynah cage is about 1.8m (6ft) long by 0.9m (3ft) wide and deep. If you are unable to obtain a suitable cage of these dimensions, the only option will be to make one. Indeed, it will probably prove considerably cheaper in any case. Melamine-covered chipboard, widely available from DIY outlets, is ideal for this purpose. Although this is rather heavy, it has the advantage that the surface can be wiped over regularly, making it easy to keep the interior of the cage clean from day to day.

Once you have constructed the basic box, seal all the joints with a thin covering of aquarium silicone sealant to protect any cut edge of

Above: This type of cage is usually too small for a pet mynah bird, which is naturally very active. Ideally, make a much larger one.

the chipboard from water and also to close off any gaps where parasites might lurk. Make the front frame of the unit with 2.5cm (1in) square timber. As mynah birds are not destructive, 19-gauge (19G) mesh will be adequate for the front of their enclosure. To improve its appearance in the home, use green plastic-coated mesh rather than standard galvanized type.

At least one door is required for access to the cage. This can either be positioned at one end or, preferably, fitted into the wire-mesh front. If the door is located in the centre of the mesh this will provide easy access to the whole of the interior. Construct a wooden frame to take the door and ideally arrange for the door to open downwards by fitting a hinge along the lowest edge of the frame. This will enable you to reach into the interior of the cage without difficulty.

Make up the cage front and door frame separately before fixing them into the main body of the flight. Before attaching the mesh, you can paint the wood with emulsion paint, either in white to match the coated chipboard or in a contrasting shade. Next, attach the mesh on to what will form the internal face of the framework. Take steps to prevent

Mynah cage

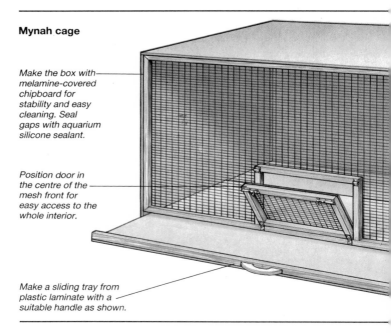

Make the box with melamine-covered chipboard for stability and easy cleaning. Seal gaps with aquarium silicone sealant.

Position door in the centre of the mesh front for easy access to the whole interior.

Make a sliding tray from plastic laminate with a suitable handle as shown.

the possibility of loose ends of wire causing injury to the bird inside. Netting staples are ideal for attaching the mesh, and to cover the loose ends of wire, attach thin battening on the faces of the framework and paint over these to complete the finish. Once all the wood is dry, fit the framework into the flight and screw it firmly in place.

Remember to allow a gap of approximately 2.5cm (1in) between the bottom of the frame and the base of the enclosure, to take a sliding tray. Use a sheet of melamine or similar plastic laminate for this and attach a length of 2.5cm (1in) timber along the front. Fix a handle to this and ensure that the tray pulls out smoothly by planing the timber if necessary.

Breeding cages
Finches can be kept in cages of similar design or, alternatively, a breeding cage which may have a nestbox attached. Indeed, if you want to try to breed these birds, it is best to keep them in a box-type cage. You can make this yourself, using special cage fronts which are available in various sizes.

Alternatively, you can buy such cages ready built from larger pet stores and bird farms. Opt for a 'double-breeding' cage if possible, since this will be more versatile, especially if it has a removable centre partition. Young birds can then be separated in one half, while their parents rear a second round of chicks on the other side.

If you do decide to build a cage of this type, it will not be necessary to use melamine-coated chipboard as suggested for a flight cage to house mynah birds. Indeed, for finches, hardboard on a wooden frame is suitable to form the basis of the box unit and the sliding tray on the cage floor. You can paint this with emulsion paint of a light shade on the inside, and with gloss paint on the outside if you wish.

Similar cages can be used for breeding canaries, although the fronts tend to differ somewhat in their design. Budgerigars, in view of their more destructive natures, are best housed in breeding cages made of plywood. A hole for the nestbox may be cut in one end, with the box being held in place externally by a suitable bracket.

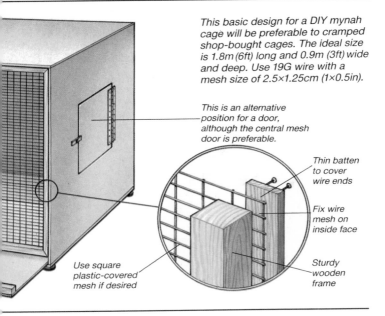

This basic design for a DIY mynah cage will be preferable to cramped shop-bought cages. The ideal size is 1.8m (6ft) long and 0.9m (3ft) wide and deep. Use 19G wire with a mesh size of 2.5×1.25cm (1×0.5in).

This is an alternative position for a door, although the central mesh door is preferable.

Thin batten to cover wire ends

Fix wire mesh on inside face

Sturdy wooden frame

Use square plastic-covered mesh if desired

Larger flight cages

Clearly, constructing an enclosure for parrots is likely to be much more costly, and the resulting structure may appear rather unattractive. Yet it is possible to overcome this

Below: *A typical 'double-breeding' cage, housing canaries in this instance. Note the containers positioned outside the cage front.*

difficulty if you can locate a supplier of individual mesh panels, which you can simply clip together to form a flight cage. Systems of this type are very versatile and easy to expand at a later date. Such flexibility is ideal when introducing one parrot to another; the birds can be kept apart at first, and then later, the two cages amalgamated to form a larger flight area.

The manufacturers of such systems advertise in the more specialist birdkeeping magazines, but their products have yet to make significant inroads into the traditional pet store. This seems surprising, since the flatpacks containing the various components would seem an attractive commercial proposition, compared with the relatively large area required for the storage and display of traditional cages.

Cleaning and floor coverings
Before you buy a cage, look to see how easy it will be to clean. The commonest arrangement is a sliding tray that slots into the base. In practice, although these trays usually fit flush on the floor of the base unit, debris tends to accumulate around the sides. You will need to open the door, therefore, to clean the interior thoroughly. As an alternative, the whole base of certain cages, especially those suitable for budgerigars and canaries, can be separated from the upper part, enabling the tray to be removed at the same time. Although it is relatively easy to keep such cages very clean, the bird may escape from underneath, especially when you are removing or replacing the base unit. The plastic used to form the base may be translucent or totally opaque. Birds generally seem to find the latter type less disconcerting.

A variety of materials can be used to cover the floor of the cage, sandsheets being most popular. These are only available in certain sizes however, corresponding to the most popular cage designs.

An alternative is loose sand, which can be bought in packeted form and is simply spread over the dirt tray in the cage. Unfortunately, this tends to prove messy, and can end up being scattered into the room. It is not particularly absorbent and may cause irritation, especially to hen budgerigars being kept on their own without nesting facilities. Such birds may attempt to form a nest on the floor of the cage, and even lay eggs there. The sand can penetrate the hen's vent area, where it will cause discomfort.

Sand is also relatively bulky, especially in the quantities required to cover the floor of a parrot cage. However, it can be used in conjunction with newspaper, when less will be required. Newspaper itself is very absorbent, and so makes an ideal cage lining. It is particularly good for coping with the liquid droppings of mynah birds. Do not use coloured sheets, as these could contain toxic substances; all birds will chew the floor covering of their cage and so are liable to be affected by harmful chemicals in this way. Newspaper may be unsightly, but it is easy to fold and fit into any cage, remaining in place unless disturbed by the bird. It is also cheap and easy to dispose of, enabling you to clean the base of the cage more easily than with sand alone, which sticks to the tray when it becomes wet. A good working compromise, therefore, is to use a thick layer of newspaper sheets 'camouflaged' with sand.

Provided that the cage is equipped with a removable dirt tray, there is really no need to use any floor covering at all. A simple layer of paper will make cleaning easier, however, and paper towelling is a good alternative to newspaper for this purpose. There are various proprietary floor coverings available, but do ensure that these are neither toxic nor likely to turn mouldy when wet. The possibility of mould developing is also a good reason for not using hay or straw as a lining material in a bird cage.

Some older designs of parrot cage incorporate a false wire floor above the dirt tray. This should be removed, primarily because the bird could trap its foot or leg in the mesh, but also because it will hamper cleaning. Parrot droppings tend to adhere to the wire, rather than falling through onto the dirt tray beneath. This means that you will need to remove and wash the grid every day, to ensure that it remains clean. Good hygiene is vital for a caged bird, since it may drop food onto the

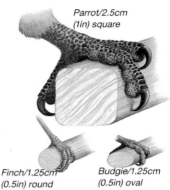

Parrot/2.5cm
(1in) square

Finch/1.25cm
(0.5in) round

Budgie/1.25cm
(0.5in) oval

Above: *Provide parrots with branches to gnaw, otherwise their beaks can become overgrown, and they may start feather plucking.*

Above: *Ideal perch size and shape vary with different birds. Most parrots need 2.5cm (1in) diameter; half this suits smaller birds.*

floor and then descend to pick it up. Clearly, the bird will be at serious risk if the floor covering is very dirty or mouldy.

Perches
It is essential to provide adequate perching facilities. Cages are now often sold equipped with plastic perches. However, these are uncomfortable for many birds, and do not give parrots the same opportunity to exercise their beaks as do wooden perches. Gnawing not only helps to keep the beak in trim, but also serves to occupy the bird, so that it is less likely to resort to pulling its feathers out. Although a parrot may not show any immediate aversion to a plastic perch, it will often refuse to use the perch within a few weeks, preferring to cling to the sides of the cage.

You can offer a variety of natural branches as alternatives, but ensure that none shows any signs of mould or fungi, which could prove harmful. Indeed, it is better to cut the branches from a living tree, rather than using dead and rotting wood. Having cut the branches, remove any leaves and trim off any side-shoots as necessary. Before cutting them to size, wash the branches thoroughly in case they have been soiled by wild birds, which could present a health threat to your pet. For the same reason, avoid any

which have been sprayed with chemicals, since these could have an adverse effect on birds gnawing the wood.

Fruit trees, such as apple, are popular for perches. Sycamore is a relatively hard wood that grows quite straight, so that it can be easily cut to fit into a cage. Elder also has a straight growth, but tends to be destroyed quite rapidly, so you will need a regular supply of branches.

The ideal diameter of the perches depends largely on the species concerned. Most parrots can perch comfortably on branches which are about 2.5cm (1in) or so in diameter, whereas budgerigars and canaries are quite happy with perches about 1.25cm (0.5in) in width. Some variation in diameter, though, is recommended, to prevent the build-up of pressure points on the feet. Budgerigars provided only with dowelling perches of a regular diameter often suffer in this way. The pressure points, seen at first as swellings on the undersurface of the feet, may become infected, and invariably this will be worse in obese budgerigars. If you choose to use dowel, avoid this problem by planing some perches flat at the top and bottom, thus offering the bird some variation in grip.

Finches can develop similar symptoms, and will do best if you provide them with fresh twigs;

replace these regularly as they dry out and become hard. Dowelling for finches should be less than 1.25cm (0.5in) in diameter.

Mynah birds create a special problem in that they tend to soil their perches with their relatively watery droppings. They also hop about on the floor of their cage, getting their feet dirty as a result. They will also wipe their beaks along a perch, spreading sticky fruit juice, for example, in the process. Therefore, it is vital to wash or change their perches regularly to prevent foot infections developing.

The number of perches required in a cage will vary, according to the dimensions of the enclosure. Most parrot cages only have sufficient space for one perch to be included although, in some cases, it may be possible to fit two. Ensure that these do not overhang, or the lower perch will become soiled. Avoid positioning perches directly above open food and water pots for the same reason. In a flight, hang perches across the enclosure rather than lengthways, so that the birds can fly up and down without obstruction.

Fixing perches in place
Perches can be fixed in place in various ways. With dowelling or a relatively straight piece of branch, it may be possible simply to cut notches at either end and to use these to support it against the bars in the cage.

A different approach is required in a box-type cage. It may be possible to hold the branches in place with a netting staple at the front of the cage and a screw attaching the perch to the solid back panel. The main problem with this method is that the branch tends to split, and the weight of a mynah bird – which is relatively heavy – could be sufficient to bring the perch down. Glue, carefully applied to the cut end, can be useful but this will prevent removal of the perch for cleaning. The best solution may be to fit a wooden notch at the back of the cage to support the perch and to fix a loop of wire at the front of the perch so that it can be

Above: *Parrots at liberty in the room can be trained to sit on a T-stand, with a droppings tray beneath forming part of the base.*

hooked onto the wire mesh. This allows the perches to be unhooked whenever necessary.

Stands
Stands are available for most designs of cage, but whether they are worthwhile depends on where you plan to put the cage in the room. A stand may simply clutter the room unnecessarily. Many people prefer to use an existing piece of furniture, such as a table, on which to stand the cage. This often creates a more stable base in any case. Indeed, some stands are surprisingly light and easily tipped over, and are especially vulnerable in a home with other pets or young children. It is safer to avoid using a stand in these situations.

Apart from stands used to support a cage, T-shaped stands may be used as perches for some parrots, such as macaws. This gives them more space for exercise and, in the case of macaws, ensures that their relatively long tail plumes are not damaged by close confinement in a standard cage. Again stability is a key consideration. Also, ensure that the tray area on the floor is adequate to hold droppings and discarded food such as seed husks and uneaten fruit.

A T-stand is suitable for a very tame parrot, which is accustomed to its owner's presence and will not try to fly off when approached. The bird can be chained to the stand, using one of the special leg rings marketed for this purpose. However, this cannot be recommended as a method of restraining an untamed bird, especially in a home with young children. If the bird is frightened, it may attempt to fly and is likely to end up dangling from the end of the chain. Also, if a leg ring is not fitted correctly it is liable to injure the bird's leg.

Secondhand cages

Old cages are occasionally offered for sale, and good examples can command high prices, sometimes purely as decorative ornaments. They are frequently of more durable construction than their modern counterparts, and any damage can often be repaired without showing too much. More modern cages are also offered for sale through newspaper advertisements at relatively low cost, and these may be suitable for housing a new occupant.

Do try to discover the fate of the previous occupant if possible, though, since some infectious diseases can be transmitted via the fabric of a cage. In any event, strip the cage down and wash all the components thoroughly in detergent to remove any obvious dirt. Then immerse the parts in a solution of disinfectant at the strength recommended by the manufacturer. Be sure to rinse everything thoroughly, so that no trace of disinfectant remains on the cage or its accessories. Once it has dried, reassemble the cage; it should now be safe for another bird.

Avoid buying any cages that show signs of rust, especially if the bars are affected. The particles of rust may enter the mouth of any parrot-like birds, including budgerigars, and will be swallowed. The particles may damage the lining of the crop, which acts as a storage organ for seed, and may even penetrate the crop wall, creating serious problems.

Older parrot cages frequently include brass fitments. Unfortunately, these often show signs of verdigris – also described as 'green rust' – because of the presence of copper in this alloy. Since verdigris is toxic, it is vital to clean or replace any affected fitments. The various individual cage components are available from the larger avicultural suppliers, by mail order if necessary, so that replacing these items should not prove difficult.

Positioning the cage

Although you should keep your bird in the room where you will spend most time, never consider the kitchen for this purpose. Fumes, notably those from non stick cooking utensils which overheat, can prove fatal to your pet in a confined air space. In addition, seed husks are liable to contaminate your cooking and tend to be harder to clear up in the confines of a kitchen than in other rooms.

Place the cage close to a wall, in order to give the bird a sense of security. A corner of the room is ideal for this purpose. Ensure that the site is not exposed to sunlight, as this may well be harmful, if not fatal, to your bird. Although parrots, for example, are found in tropical areas, they avoid the direct rays of the sun, tending to feed during the morning and evening when the temperature is lower. Signs of heatstroke include panting and a faster breathing rate than normal. Distressed birds can die rapidly unless they are immediately transferred to a cooler spot.

Heatstroke may also occur in birds kept in a conservatory during the summer months. This is not a good location in any event because of the rapid rise in temperature during the day followed by the equally rapid fall that can occur at night. Such dramatic changes are likely to affect the bird's moulting pattern, if nothing else.

Aim to place the cage at about eye-level. This will enable you to tame the bird more easily, and should ensure that the bird feels relatively secure, having a good view around the room. It will also make cleaning the cage easier and more convenient. However, you may have to watch out for children who, in their enthusiasm to reach the bird, might pull the cage down. As a precaution, if the cage is positioned against the wall, consider fixing up some hooks to secure it in place.

Bringing your new pet home
Birds generally travel better in boxes than in cages and are less likely to damage their plumage if transported in this way. While it is safe to move budgerigars, canaries or finches in cardboard boxes, it is much better to transport parrots in wooden containers, in view of their more destructive habits.

Be sure to provide adequate ventilation during the journey. To prepare a cardboard box, for transporting a bird, simply punch holes in the sides using a pair of scissors. This should allow sufficient air circulation once the bird is inside. Take care not to make the holes too large; some birds, particularly budgerigars, may use them as a starting point to gnaw their way out. Mynah birds, although not destructive in this way, can nevertheless puncture the sides of a thin cardboard box. Thus, for these birds use a relatively robust container that can be adequately sealed for the journey home.

Ask the vendor beforehand whether you should supply your own box. Most pet stores and other trade outlets will provide a carrying box, but they may charge you for this, especially for a wooden container suitable for larger birds.

It can be useful to take your own cage with you, particularly if the base can be separated easily from the mesh framework. If you choose a carrying box that is large enough for your bird but small enough to fit inside the cage, you can simply assemble the cage around the box with the bird inside. This ensures that even if the bird does escape from its box, there is no risk of it being lost during the journey. Once safely indoors, you can simply remove the box and reassemble the cage before releasing the bird inside it to settle down.

After obtaining your bird, always take the most direct route home, to minimize travelling time. There is

Above: *Birds travel best in boxes. Here a budgerigar is being placed in a cardboard carrier. Other parrots require wooden boxes.*

generally no need to worry about providing food for a relatively short journey. However, if the bird is being sent by rail, it is usual to provide seed and diced apple in the box, the latter providing a source of fluid during the journey. If you have a long drive home, it may be best to leave in the late afternoon, when the bird is likely to have eaten. Travelling during the hours of darkness will cause the minimum of disturbance. There is always a slight risk of digestive problems arising with newly weaned parrots if they are deprived of the opportunity to feed adequately during the day.

Never transport the bird in the boot of your car, since exhaust fumes may penetrate and build up in this area, with fatal consequences. Similarly, do not park and leave the bird in its box in the car on a hot day. The temperature within the vehicle will rise very rapidly and, even out of direct sunlight, the bird may die from the effects of heatstroke.

While a car offers the best transport, it is usually possible to move your bird by other means, including bus and train. Regulations vary, so check beforehand, especially if you are carrying a parrot. Although usually quiet once they are in darkened surroundings, these birds can still prove noisy on occasions and may upset fellow passengers nervous about birds.

Below: *Choosing a cage in a local pet store. Be sure to select a practical, spacious cage; this one offers restricted flying space.*

Feeding

All the species covered in this book are relatively easy to feed. Indeed, the majority will accept seed as the major item in their diet, although other items such as fruit should be offered on a regular basis.

Types of seed

The seeds used as bird food can be divided broadly into two categories: cereal and oil. The cereals contain a relatively high level of carbohydrate, compared with their oil (fat) content. Seeds of this type include plain canary seed, millets, maize and groats (oat kernels). In contrast, oil seeds are rich in fat and low in carbohydrate. Common oil seeds include sunflower seed, peanuts, safflower, pine nuts, rape, maw, niger and linseed.

The other major ingredient of both groups of seed is protein, which is made up of individual amino acid residues. Although the protein level of a seed may be high, this does not necessarily mean that the bird is receiving an adequate protein intake. It may be that all the amino acids are not present in adequate quantities, and the bird is not able to manufacture those essential residues which are in short supply. Typically, birds are likely to be deficient in the amino acids known as lysine and methonine. It is now possible to provide these separately in a synthetic form, however, as a food supplement.

As well as being low on certain vital amino acids, seed also tends to be a poor source of minerals and some vitamins, such as Vitamin A. Vitamin A deficiency may well be a contributory factor towards the disease candidiasis. This can give rise to white fungus-like spots in the mouth, and may spread through the digestive tract if not treated. Young birds, both hand reared and imported, are most susceptible.

One of the earliest signs of the disease is that the bird starts to play with its food but actually swallows very little. Although this can also be associated with other ailments, notably sour crop in budgerigars, look for the signs of candidiasis. Again, it is possible to provide a Vitamin A supplement, although it is preferable to rely on a balanced diet with higher levels of Vitamin A.

Below: *A selection of pure seeds which are commonly used as bird food. Some may be available only from specialist suppliers. Whenever purchasing seed, check that it appears clean, like these samples. It is impossible to assess the nutritional value of seed without expensive tests but, if fresh, it should germinate well.*

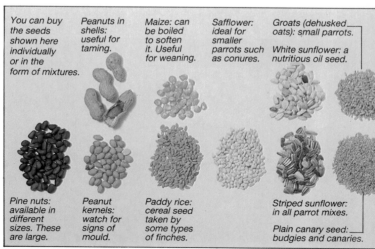

You can buy the seeds shown here individually or in the form of mixtures.

Peanuts in shells: useful for taming.

Maize: can be boiled to soften it. Useful for weaning.

Safflower: ideal for smaller parrots such as conures.

Groats (dehusked oats): small parrots.

White sunflower: a nutritious oil seed.

Pine nuts: available in different sizes. These are large.

Peanut kernels: watch for signs of mould.

Paddy rice: cereal seed taken by some types of finches.

Striped sunflower: in all parrot mixes.

Plain canary seed: budgies and canaries.

Seed diets

Budgerigars are usually offered a combination of plain canary seed and millet. Canary seed is grown in different countries around the world and yet still known under the one name, whereas the various types of millet are recognized by different names. Probably the most popular is panicum, which is available loose or as a seedhead, described as a 'spray'. Other millets which may be found in budgerigar food include pearl white and Japanese millets. Not all forms are popular, however; most budgerigars do not favour red millet, leaving this until last in any mixture.

Most owners prefer to buy seed ready mixed, although you can buy the ingredients separately and blend them together at home if you wish. Seed is available either loose or in packeted form and, as a general rule, you will find that the packeted seed is less dusty. When assessing any sample, check first that it is not dirty and flows freely through the hand. If there are any signs of dampness or germination, or evidence of mouse droppings, you should reject the seed. Most suppliers are rigorous in maintaining the quality of their seed, but occasionally problems do arise. It is important to be careful because poor seed could have a very detrimental effect on your pet's health in the long term.

Parrot food

The ingredients in a typical parrot mixture vary, but sunflower seed invariably predominates. The striped variety is most often present, although the white form is more valuable since it contains a higher level of protein and relatively less fat. If you are buying sunflower seed loose, choose the smaller grades. Although the larger forms of sunflower seeds may appear to offer the best value, in reality the reverse is true, since the parrot discards the outer husk and the inner kernel does not vary much in size in relation to the outer hull.

A seed that is sometimes confused with white sunflower, but is significantly smaller and more rotund in outline, is safflower. This is a particular favourite of many conures and other smaller parakeets.

A relative newcomer to parrot mixtures – and taken readily by most species – is the pine nut. These vary quite considerably in size and are graded accordingly. Watch for any chipped nuts; these can be affected with a bright greenish blue mould and must be discarded. Supplies can be unpredictable, however, since pine

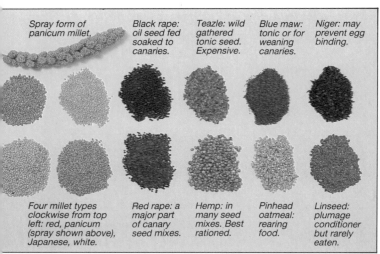

Spray form of panicum millet.

Black rape: oil seed fed soaked to canaries.

Teazle: wild gathered tonic seed. Expensive.

Blue maw: tonic or for weaning canaries.

Niger: may prevent egg binding.

Four millet types clockwise from top left: red, panicum (spray shown above), Japanese, white.

Red rape: a major part of canary seed mixes.

Hemp: in many seed mixes. Best rationed.

Pinhead oatmeal: rearing food.

Linseed: plumage conditioner but rarely eaten.

nuts are gathered wild to supply the birdfood market and are not cultivated as are the majority of other seeds.

Be particularly careful if you feed parrots with peanuts, either loose or in their shells. There is a mould that attacks these nuts, producing potent toxins that are likely to have severe effects on the liver. These toxins will almost certainly prove fatal over a period of time.

While oil seeds usually predominate in a parrot mix, cereals are also generally included. One of these may be maize, in either whole or kibbled (ground) form. Maize is very hard in its dry state, however, and can be cracked only by birds with powerful beaks. It is thus rarely eaten by the smaller parakeets, which prefer to take groats.

Canary food

Canaries usually receive a diet of both cereals and oil seeds. Most mixtures contain a combination of plain canary seed and red rape, to which other seeds have been added in smaller quantities. These include hemp, an oil seed which is also very popular with parrotlike birds. It is traditionally fed in greater quantities during the winter months to birds living in outdoor aviaries, since it is a concentrated energy source. Canaries, which are messy feeders, will frequently empty their food pot over the floor of the cage in the search for any hemp seeds buried towards the bottom.

Linseed, a flat, oval, brown seed, never attracts such attention, and is usually ignored by most canaries. It is said to be particularly valuable during the moulting phase, however, helping to ensure that the new plumage develops a healthy 'bloom' or shine. Canary fanciers also favour increasing the relative amounts of other seeds at certain times of the year. Just before the breeding season, for example, fanciers may give niger and teazle as 'conditioning' seeds. Niger, a distinctive, black rodlike seed, is said to help guard against eggbinding. Blue maw, a tiny seed obtained from poppies, is widely used for the successful weaning of young canaries. It is also taken readily by older birds, and is often described as a 'tonic' seed.

Soaked and sprouted seed

While birds should have a supply of dry seeds in front of them, they also benefit from the provision of so-

Below: *A variety of seed mixes. You can prepare these yourself or buy them ready mixed. Some mixtures can prove wasteful, so* *you may prefer to choose your own ingredients. In order to provide a balanced diet, offer your pet bird some fresh foods as well.*

British finch mix.

Canary mix: largely plain canary seed and rape.

Budgie breeder mix: more canary seed.

Parakeet mix: millets, canary seed, sunflower.

Parrot mix: includes sunflower, peanuts, maize, etc.

Foreign finch mix: more millet.

Typical budgerigar mixes: mainly millet plus canary seed.

Ideal for cockatiels, parrotlets.

Ideal for a range of parrots.

Above: *Most birds prefer to feed from a perch, as with this pet cockatiel. Food offered on the floor may be soiled by droppings. Be sure to use suitable containers.*

called 'soaked seed'. This is seed which has been immersed in warm water for about a day to stimulate the germination process, which leads to alterations in its nutritional value. Chemical changes within the seeds increase their protein value, for example. It is not surprising, therefore, that soaked seed is especially popular during the breeding and moulting periods, when the bird's protein reserves are most likely to be low.

Take care when feeding soaked seed, especially in a warm room, since it provides an ideal medium for the growth of fungi. Always pour off the water and wash the seed thoroughly in a sieve under a running tap before feeding it to your bird. Allow the seed to drain thoroughly and tip it into a separate food pot hooked onto the inside of the cage or flight. If given in the morning, remove the container in the evening and wash it thoroughly before refilling it the following morning. Clean the cage floor at the same time to ensure that no spilt soaked seed remains on the floor.

Black rape is traditionally prepared in this way for canaries, while plain canary seed and millet sprays are the cereals usually offered as soaked seeds. White or striped sunflower can also be soaked satisfactorily. Avoid soaking black sunflower seed; it releases a dye into the water which some fanciers believe to be harmful.

A recent trend among parrot keepers has been the increasing use of pulses to form part of their birds' diet. Assorted peas, beans and lentils can be soaked in water and offered as parrot food. Mung beans are now available in bulk from specialist seed merchants catering for the avicultural market, although you are unlikely to find such items at your local pet store. For a small quantity, it will probably be best to turn to your local health food store, unless you decide to order your seeds by mail from one of the specialist suppliers.

You can also offer the pulses once they have germinated and formed shoots. Sprouting units are available for this purpose. Be sure to wash the growing shoots very thoroughly before offering them to your bird. Sprouted seeds are highly perishable and should be removed before they become wilted or show any signs of mould.

Greenstuff
While most of the birds featured in this book live mainly on a seed-based diet, they will also readily take greenstuff. The availability of fresh green plants and vegetables will depend on your individual circumstances and on the time of year. If you have access to a garden, you should be able to pick greenfood for your bird throughout the year. Wild plants, notably chickweed (*Stellaria media*), will be readily taken by finches and budgerigars. Several sprigs can be offered daily, and if it grows in shady moist surroundings, chickweed will be available for much of the year. Dandelion leaves (*Taraxacum*

officinale) can also be given in moderation, and so can seeding grasses and plantains.

Offer only relatively small amounts of greenfood, however, especially if your bird is unused to it. Excessive quantities can cause diarrhoea (known as 'scouring'). Always wash all greenfood before supplying it, and avoid collecting it from locations where potentially harmful chemicals may have been used, such as roadside verges.

During periods of cold weather, when there is snow on the ground, you may still be able to provide greenstuff for your bird if you have previously planted spinach beet (*Beta vulgaris*) – also known as perpetual spinach. Varieties with low levels of oxalic acid in their leaves are preferable for birds, since this chemical can interfere with calcium absorption. While some birds prefer the leaves themselves, many parrots enjoy chewing the fleshy stems. Always allow the spinach, and indeed any greenstuff, to warm up if it has been brought in during sub-zero temperatures, before offering it to your birds. Some birds will also take cabbage, although this generally appears less popular than spinach.

The main value of greenstuff and similar items lies in their vitamin and mineral content. Such foods consist essentially of water, and are thus of little calorific value compared with seeds. Yet they do also add bulk and fibre to the diet and thus, if given on a regular basis, may help to prevent obesity.

Colouring agents

Carrot is a typical example of a colouring agent. (It is also highly valued as a source of Vitamin A). It can function as a natural colouring agent for birds, such as canaries, whose coloration is – at least in some cases – derived from their food. However, synthetic derivatives, now widely marketed, are more potent than raw carrot. The active components, described as carotenoids, can now be supplied simply by adding a prescribed quantity of a solution to the bird's

drinking water or, alternatively, using a softfood which also contains a colouring agent. This applies especially to the group of canaries described as Red Factor birds. But colour feeding is not required for parrots; they will retain their red coloration over successive moults without the need for colouring agents in their diet.

Grit

The digestive system of seed-eating birds has evolved in the absence of teeth to crack the hard kernels after the husk has been removed. Instead, the dehusked seeds are effectively ground up in an organ known as the gizzard. Here, particles of grit (in the wild, swallowed with the food) help to break down the seeds and prevent them sticking together.

Two main types of grit are important for bird nutrition: soluble and insoluble. Soluble oystershell grit dissolves quite readily in the gizzard and serves essentially as a source of minerals. The harder insoluble grits, such as flint grits, are more valuable in forming an integral part of the digestive process.

Suitable grit is obtainable in packets from your pet store, and you should always make some available, even if your bird tends not to consume a great deal. Parrots in particular may seem to take little grit, but examination of their gizzards reveals that it is usually present in this organ, and thus should be offered.

Iodine

As studies have progressed, so a better understanding of the specific nutritional needs of individual groups of birds, or even species, has been gained. It is now known that budgerigars seem to have a relatively high requirement for iodine. They should have constant access to an iodine block, available from most pet stores, which they gnaw when necessary. A deficiency of iodine may give rise to the symptoms of goitre, including a swelling of the thyroid glands in the neck. These glands, because of

Beaks for different diets

Canary

Canaries use their short conical beaks to crack seeds.

Macaw

A macaw uses its flexible tongue and powerful beak to open nuts.

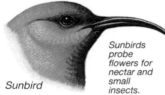

Sunbird

Sunbirds probe flowers for nectar and small insects.

Above: *Birds' beaks reflect the basic differences in their feeding habits; three representative types are shown here. Some are more powerful than others, with parrots being able to exert considerable pressure using their strong bills.*

their position, are liable to press on the windpipe if they are enlarged and thus interfere with the bird's breathing.

Cuttlefish bone

Cuttlefish bone is a traditional means of supplying calcium to seed-eating birds. These flat, white 'bones' are available from seed suppliers, and can be held in the cage by means of special clips. When approaching breeding condition, hen birds usually attack cuttlefish bone with great vigour, thereby gaining a supply of calcium for the eggshells. Finches may have

difficulty in gnawing at the bone, and will benefit if smaller pieces are cut from the powdery side.

Cuttlefishes are marine molluscs, and their 'bones' – which are really internal buoyancy chambers – may be found along the seashore. Providing these are clean, you can use them for your bird. Keep them immersed in fresh water over a period of a week or so, changing the water every day. After a final rinse, allow the bones to dry thoroughly, preferably in the sun, before storing for use when required.

Unlike foodstuffs, these bones will keep indefinitely without deteriorating. Seed, however, will decline slowly in terms of its overall nutritive value, and must be kept in a dry environment if it is not to spoil. Never purchase more than about three months' supply of seed at any time and store it carefully.

Diets for mynah birds

Mynahs are popularly classed by aviculturists as 'softbilled' birds, but this term describes their feeding habits rather than their beaks. Mynahs will not eat seed, nor do they require grit or cuttlefish. They need to be offered special softbill

Below: *Most parrots, with the exception of budgerigars, will use their feet for holding food. They may show a preference for one leg.*

food, of which many brands are now available. Some softbill foods can be used straight from the packet; others need to be mixed with water. Once a bird is used to a particular brand, do not change it suddenly, for this may cause a digestive upset. Gradually altering the diet enables the bird's system to adapt over a period of time, thus reducing the risk of adverse effects.

Softbill food may be loose and powdery in consistency, and so will adhere readily to fruit, the other major ingredient of a softbill's diet. A wide variety of different fruits can be given, although apple tends to be popular because it is widely available in most countries throughout the year. Grapes are another useful item, and are likely to be eaten whole, the pips and remnants of the skin passing through the digestive tract. When in season, grapes can be deep frozen and thawed out when required.

Orange tends to be rather acidic, and banana is not favoured by all softbill keepers, partly because it is messy and also because it may cause digestive disturbance if it is either greenish or too ripe. However, dried fruits can be safely included in softbill food, provided that they are well soaked beforehand and then thoroughly rinsed. Even canned fruit can be used if necessary, so long as it is in natural juice rather than syrup. Parrots, also, will readily take fruit.

A recent development in avian nutrition has been the preparation of pelleted diets for a wide range of species. Softbill pellets, which need to be soaked for up to an hour before feeding, are especially useful for mynah birds. While mynahs will take loose softbill food, especially when it is adhering to the cut surface of fruit, they will take pellets more readily. In combination with a ration of fruit each day, pellets provide a balanced diet for such starlings. Do

Below: *A range of fresh and processed foodstuffs. Health food stores can be a useful source of supply for nuts, pulses and dried fruits. Apart from the items shown here, a food supplement may also be recommended. If it contains the essential amino acids, as well as vitamins and minerals, it will be particularly valuable for seedeaters, and can be sprinkled over fruit or damp greenfood.*

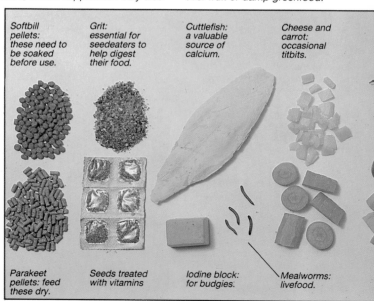

Softbill pellets: these need to be soaked before use.

Grit: essential for seedeaters to help digest their food.

Cuttlefish: a valuable source of calcium.

Cheese and carrot: occasional titbits.

Parakeet pellets: feed these dry.

Seeds treated with vitamins

Iodine block: for budgies.

Mealworms: livefood.

not feed mynah pellets exclusively, however, as this may have harmful effects over a period of time.

On a mixed diet of this type, it is not strictly necessary to offer invertebrates, such as mealworms, to your mynah bird. Mealworms are the larval form of the meal beetle (*Tenebrio molitor*). They are readily available and easy to maintain in a plastic container filled with chicken meal. Mealworms can become a nuisance, however, if they escape the mynah bird's attention and wriggle free into the room. This problem can be avoided with a tame bird if you ration the number of mealworms provided and watch while they are eaten.

Do ensure that the mealworms cannot escape from their container, by placing the lid back firmly and restricting the size of the ventilation holes. Thin slices of apple, replaced at intervals as they shrivel up, will provide adequate moisture for the mealworms, so no water is required. There is no need to clean mealworms before feeding them. They are preferable to other livefoods, such as earthworms, which are much more likely to present a threat to your pet's health.

Nectar feeders

While the majority of parrots feed on seeds and similar foods, the lories and lorikeets depend essentially on pollen and nectar to supply the basic ingredients of their diet. Pollen is rich in protein, while nectar acts as a source of carbohydrate. Although many owners of these birds still prefer to mix the nectar to their own recipes, the task of caring for nectar feeders is now greatly eased by the availability of prepared diets that contain all the necessary ingredients to keep such birds in good health. It is especially vital with nectar-feeding parrots not to alter the diet suddenly. This is likely to lead to changes in the bacterial population within the gut, which could precipitate a fatal bout of enterotoxaemia.

Before acquiring a lory or lorikeet, therefore, obtain detailed feeding instructions so that you can seek out the necessary ingredients beforehand. Nectar mixtures need to be prepared fresh each day, and the vessels used must be kept spotlessly clean. Closed drinkers are generally best, so that there is no risk of the bird mistaking the sticky solution for a bath.

Fresh fruit: appreciated by many birds.

Dried fruits: soak and rinse well before use.

Softbill food: mix with water.

Nectar powder: mix with water.

Colour food: use during moulting.

Brazils: for large parrots

Rearing and conditioning food.

Nectar paste: prepared for nectivores.

Colour food with seed.

Lories and lorikeets will also eat fruit readily, and this should be provided daily. Although some birds can adapt to a diet containing a relatively high proportion of seed, in most cases this is not to be recommended. The digestive tract of the vast majority of lories and lorikeets is simply not adapted to deal with seeds.

Water containers

A clean supply of water should always be available to your bird. Tubular drinkers that clip onto the sides of the cage or flight are ideal for budgerigars and other small birds. Unfortunately, parrots tend to destroy the plastic base of these units, and mynah birds may not find them always sufficiently accessible.

It is possible to supply water in open pots that simply hook over the front of the birds' quarters, but these can become dirty quite rapidly. Mynahs in fact are inveterate bathers, and will certainly immerse themselves in a large pot of water, scattering the contents all around the cage and over the surrounding furniture. Worse still, the remaining water in the container is liable to be soiled and rendered unfit to drink.

Providing regular bathing facilities and a relatively small pot of drinking water should help to overcome these problems. The sealed drinking bottles produced primarily for parrots may also prove acceptable to mynahs, so it could be worth investing in this option. The water is kept within a bottle to

Below: *A selection of feeding containers and drinkers. Plastic vessels are not recommended for large parrots, since they are quite capable of destroying these with their powerful beaks, and may injure themselves in the process. Galvanized metal containers are sometimes used, but check these*

first for any sharp splinters. Also avoid using them for water containing any chemicals. Glazed earthenware pots are ideal in those situations where open containers are suitable, mainly because they are heavy, chemically inert and can be cleaned easily. Check that drinking bottles are firmly fixed.

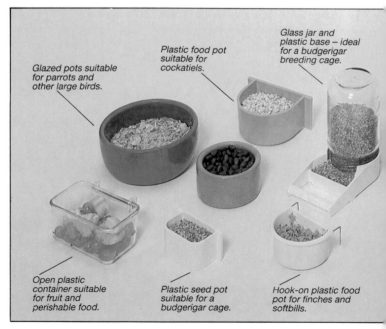

Glass jar and plastic base – ideal for a budgerigar breeding cage.

Plastic food pot suitable for cockatiels.

Glazed pots suitable for parrots and other large birds.

Open plastic container suitable for fruit and perishable food.

Plastic seed pot suitable for a budgerigar cage.

Hook-on plastic food pot for finches and softbills.

avoid contamination, while the stainless steel spout contains two small balls that serve as the reservoir control. When the bird pushes the first ball back, the vacuum is broken and water flows through the spout.

Unfortunately, such drinkers are held in place on the outside of the cage simply by a loop of wire. Parrots, especially, will soon learn to undo this hook, and the bottle may fall to the floor and break. It is best to provide an additional fastening or, alternatively, to twist the ends of the wire with pliers to ensure that they can only be undone in a similar fashion. If you discover that the bottle has leaked, it is likely that the spout is not fixed securely into the bottle.

While these containers are ideal for supplying water, they are not suitable for nectar. The spout is difficult to clean, and if the nectar contains particles in suspension these will tend to precipitate out at the bottom of the vessel. A broad-spouted container, usually marketed as a seed hopper, is more suitable as a nectar feeder.

Food supplements

The most satisfactory food supplements are those containing not only vitamins, minerals and trace elements, but also the range of amino acids mentioned previously, including lysine. Check the pack for the precise formulation. Some of these products are available in powder form, whereas others need to be given in drinking water.

Never overdose supplements of any kind, since this could be harmful, particularly in the long term. These preparations have a limited shelf life, and so if you only have one bird, one of the smaller packs will prove less wasteful.

Supplements can be used for all birds, but are likely to be of most value to seedeaters. Alternatively, you can try to obtain a pelleted diet for seedeaters that contains all such ingredients, although unfortunately such diets are not widely available at present. They also tend not to be very palatable. Nevertheless, it will be well worth persevering if you have a young, hand-raised parrot, for such birds can be persuaded to sample such foods.

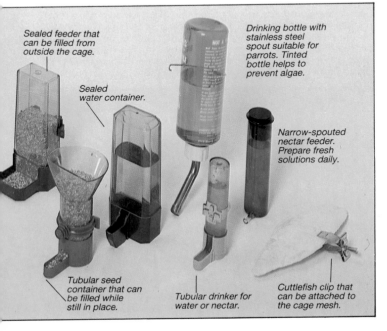

Sealed feeder that can be filled from outside the cage.

Sealed water container.

Drinking bottle with stainless steel spout suitable for parrots. Tinted bottle helps to prevent algae.

Narrow-spouted nectar feeder. Prepare fresh solutions daily.

Tubular seed container that can be filled while still in place.

Tubular drinker for water or nectar.

Cuttlefish clip that can be attached to the cage mesh.

Caring for your bird

Once your bird is established in its new quarters, leave it to settle down, keeping a close watch on its appetite and droppings to ensure that all is well. At first, after the journey home, the droppings may be rather greenish, but they should revert to normal within a day or so.

The early stages
It is important to leave the bird on its own for an hour or so after you place it in its quarters. Do not switch off the light if it is dark, since the bird will not feed without light. For mynahs, cut fruit into small pieces, since they are not able to chew off pieces in the same way as parrots.

The positioning of the food in the bird's quarters can have a distinct bearing on how readily it shows signs of eating. Most birds have an inherent dislike of descending to the ground in order to obtain food, and will be reluctant to do so in an unfamiliar cage. Initially, therefore, it is best to place food containers alongside a perch if possible. Remember that, although the young

Below: *Hand raising young cockatoos using a teaspoon with bent edges. Such birds can develop into very tame pets. It is best to wait until they are feeding on their own, however, before moving them to a new home, as problems can arise.*

birds will be weaned, it is likely this will be the first time they have been on their own.

If your budgerigar cage has covered food pots, sprinkle seed on the floor close to the pot to attract the bird to this spot. A millet spray positioned alongside a perch is usually taken quite readily, even if the budgerigar is unsure about feeding on the floor at first.

You may find that a hand-reared parrot continues to beg for food, even though it is capable of feeding itself. For the first few days, therefore, it may be preferable to feed it on the rearing mixture it has been used to, to ensure that it receives adequate sustenance over this period. Never offer a young parrot hot food; even if you heat it beforehand, allow it to cool down before feeding it. Mix the food fresh for each feed and ensure that none remains on the bird's beak afterwards, as this can cause malformation in time. A teaspoon with its edges bent inwards to form a trough makes a useful feeding tool for a young parrot.

Unfortunately, the weaning period can prove troublesome, as the parrot may beg for food but refuse the hand-feeding mixture when it is offered. If possible, take the parrot out of the cage before offering food in this way. This will make it easier to clean up rejected

food afterwards. In a cage, the food is likely to end up smeared all over the bars, and then the only effective way to clean the cage thoroughly is to wash it off, using a hose or running tap.

Catching and handling

While you can release your new pet into its quarters from its box without having to handle it, it is likely that, before long, you will need to be able to catch and restrain your bird. It is advisable to wear gloves for this purpose, particularly when dealing with parrotlike birds, for their powerful beaks are capable of inflicting a nasty bite.

Choose smooth-textured gloves, so that the bird cannot get its claws caught up in the material when being handled. Woollen or towelling gloves can prove hazardous for this reason. Stout gardening gauntlets are to be recommended for the largest parrots. While tame birds will not usually attempt to bite when they are not restrained, they are capable of using their powerful beaks to devastating effect when held in the hand.

The best way of restraining a small parrot is to hold its head gently between the first two fingers of the left hand, with the wings tucked into the palm of the hand. The remaining fingers and thumb can be used to support the rest of the body. In this position, the bird should not attempt to struggle, and most of its body will be easily accessible for you to make a close examination of the feet, for example. Support the neck gently, however, and never press hard here; this is liable to compress the windpipe and restrict the bird's breathing, perhaps with fatal results. Small birds are very frail.

If you are left-handed, simply use your right hand rather than your left to hold the bird. With the largest parrots, notably the big macaws, you will probably need both hands to restrain the bird adequately. Conversely, with canaries and finches, which will not bite, you can simply hold the bird with its head in the circle formed by your first finger and thumb. Mynahs can prove more difficult to hold, since they can peck quite painfully if they are permitted to do so. Always keep your face well away from these birds when handling them.

Catching an escapee

One of the most difficult situations that can arise is the accidental escape of a bird into a room, which may happen when you are cleaning out its quarters. The risks can be minimized by always taking the precautions recommended on pages 47-49 when letting a bird out into a room. Finches are notoriously hard to catch when flying around a room, so you may decide to have a catching net available, which should be well padded around its rim. A catching net is not very suitable for use within the average room, however, filled with ornaments, plants and furniture.

The best method of catching a loose bird is to draw the curtains and, with the room in darkness, to move round carefully to where the bird is resting. A finch may be simply cupped in your hands. Wear gloves, of course, if you are faced with a parrot that refuses to return to its cage.

Chasing the bird around the room is likely to prove distressing for it. If, in spite of all your endeavours, you cannot catch the escapee easily, and it starts breathing very heavily, leave it alone to recover. Otherwise, the stress could prove fatal, especially in hot weather.

Taming your bird

Ideally, do not let your bird out of the cage until the taming process is quite well advanced. The training of any bird is a two-way interaction, and your bird will not become tame quickly if you are unable to spend much time with it. Young birds are naturally quite tame, however, especially if they are hand reared and used to human company.

From the start, encourage the bird to feed from your hand at every opportunity, offering titbits such as pieces of fruit through the cage bars. It may be hesitant at first, but it will soon come to accept your

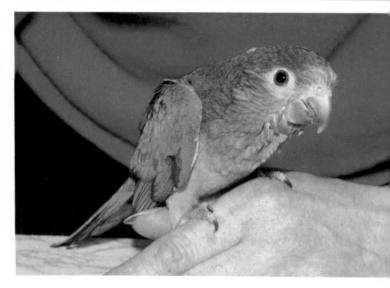

Above: *It is much easier to start training a young bird, especially one which has been hand reared and therefore has no fear of perching on your hand. Be patient.*

offerings, especially if they are given at about the same time every day. Indeed, establishing a routine is an important part of the training process.

Once the bird is feeding readily from your hand through the bars, the next stage is to hold the fruit inside the cage. Offer a slightly larger piece now, so that the bird does not have to advance too

closely at first. In fact, it is likely to withdraw to the back of the cage. You can hold the fruit relatively near to its beak, but if it still shows no inclination to feed, withdraw for the time being. Then offer the titbit again from outside the cage to re-establish the existing routine and try again at a later date.

Certain individuals prove more adventurous than others, and these birds will obviously become tame more quickly. Recently fledged birds are likely to perch quite readily on a finger. You can encourage a youngster by extending your index finger along the perch and then,

Below: *From its perch, you may be able to encourage your parrot to transfer to your shoulder. This bird is an Orange-winged Amazon.*

Below: *Encourage your parrot to rest on a perch out of its cage. Dowelling is ideal, but cut a length which you can handle easily.*

Clipping a bird's wing
Hold the wing open and cut across the feathers as shown. Leave the outermost primaries intact.

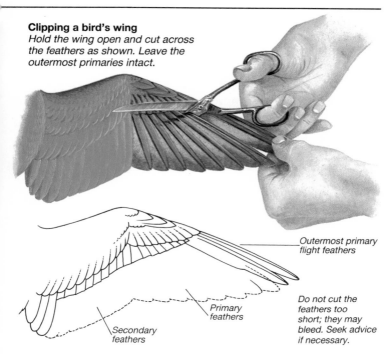

Outermost primary flight feathers

Primary feathers

Secondary feathers

Do not cut the feathers too short; they may bleed. Seek advice if necessary.

slowly and gently, moving the finger up and over the perch. The bird will change its grip, and should transfer its feet, at least in part, on to your outstretched finger. Most birds are unlikely to bite at this stage, even if they do not accept the presence of your hand in the cage. Nevertheless, it may be advisable to wear a glove, since the claws of parrots can be surprisingly sharp, especially if they grip tightly.

Wing clipping
It should then be possible to encourage your pet to perch on one hand and to feed from the other hand. Once this stage has been reached, you can consider allowing the bird out into the room. At this point, if not before, you will have to decide whether or not you want to clip your bird's wing. By restricting its powers of flight in this way you can reduce the risk of the bird injuring itself once it is free in the room. Wing clipping is, of course, a temporary measure, since the feathers will be replaced in their full splendour at the next moult.

If you are uncertain how to clip the wing, obtain advice beforehand. You will find it helpful to have an assistant, who can concentrate on holding the bird. Hold the wing open and use a sharp pair of scissors to cut carefully across the flight feathers, leaving the two outermost primary feathers in place so that the clipping does not appear too conspicuous. Cut to just above the base of the shaft. Make sure you do not cut down to the bases of the feathers, since this could cause serious bleeding. Wing clipping is a painless procedure, but the bird is likely to be somewhat withdrawn for a short period afterwards, mainly because of the unaccustomed handling it has received.

Letting your bird out
Several potential dangers exist in most rooms for birds. Clearly, open fires, or indeed flames of any kind, are highly dangerous for a bird free in the room. Other pets can also present a hazard. Cats present an obvious threat, especially if they slip into the room undetected.

Above: *Try to avoid letting your bird touch your mouth directly; it may not be hygienic. Indeed, many budgerigars will eat their own droppings in order to obtain essential B-group vitamins.*

Below: *Try to allow your pet bird to take plenty of exercise whenever possible. This will not only prevent obesity but also help it to enjoy a long and active life.*

Uncovered fish tanks can be especially dangerous. Be sure to close the windows and cover them with mesh curtains, so that the bird can see a physical obstacle and will not attempt to fly through the glass.

Parrots are especially vulnerable because of their gnawing habits. Live electrical flexes represent a special danger for such birds. Remember that if your bird actually bites through a flex, you must not

touch it until you have switched off the power supply and removed the plug from the socket, or you too run the risk of being electrocuted. A surprising number of houseplants are also potentially fatal if eaten by pet birds. It is best to remove these from the room, along with valuable ornaments, before letting the bird out of its cage.

Once a parrot is used to perching on the hand and to being let out into the room, it will happily sit on its owner's shoulder. Take care, especially at first, not to risk upsetting the bird by any sudden movement. Parrots will not usually deliberately injure their owner, although they may be attracted to strands of hair. If you are nervous, simply restrict the parrot to perching on your forearm. Never encourage it to take food directly from your mouth, since it may cut your lip or even your tongue, badly. In addition, you may transmit an infection to your pet, or vice-versa.

Once well established, it is not unusual for a tame parrot to invite its owner to scratch the sides of its head close to the back of the neck, by sitting with its head slightly on one side and its feathers raised.

Budgerigars and cockatiels tend to be more active in a room than other parrots, and perches can be located at various points around the room. The easiest way to fix perches to the walls is with suction pads, which will cause no harm to the decor. Of course, if the pads dry out, they are likely to fall off the wall.

Mimicry
Some species appear to find it easier to mimic the human voice than others, and even individuals of the same species vary in their ability to imitate sounds.

Part of the reason may be traced back to their teachers. Birds generally seem to learn better from women and children, although they can be taught by men. One of the key things to remember is never to rush the training process. Pick out the phrase or sound that you want the bird to learn and repeat this regularly at every opportunity. For

Above: *Keep birds away from human drinks, especially those of an alcoholic nature. A drop may be a stimulant; more could be fatal.*

example, saying 'Good morning' when you first enter the room each day will encourage the bird to begin to mimic these words, associating them with this time of day. Whole phrases can be taught in a similar way, by breaking them down into component parts. Repeat the words slowly and distinctly, preferably when there is no one else in the room to distract the bird's attention.

There are really no shortcuts to

Below: *Recognized as one of the best mimics in the bird kingdom, the Greater Hill Mynah will usually talk freely, even in front of strangers. Parrots, however, tend to be relatively shy about talking.*

teaching a bird to mimic words successfully, although using tapes may help to reinforce the learning process. This is especially effective if you record your own voice. Commercially produced tapes are invariably less successful, certainly with parrots, since the voice on the tape will be unknown to them. Without anyone present in the room to encourage it, the parrot generally proves less responsive. Yet it is well worth investing time in teaching a telephone number or even your address to your pet. If the bird escapes at a later date, anyone finding it will be able to track you down.

Mynah birds are excellent mimics of household sounds, such as a ringing telephone, even to the point where their calls may be confused with those of an actual telephone. This can be disconcerting and may prove rather annoying over a period of time. The only option is to move the bird to another part of the house and hope that the sound will fade from its vocabulary when it is no longer heard. Scolding the bird will have no beneficial effect, and is simply likely to damage the bond between pet and owner.

Misconceptions about mimicry

Although it is widely assumed that only cock birds can be taught to talk, especially in the case of budgerigars, this is not true. Indeed, hens can prove less talented mimics, while in the case of the larger parrots, the gender of any individual may well be unknown in any case.

Another popular myth is that a mirror in a cage will prevent the bird from talking, since it sees its own reflection and thus only uses its natural calls. This is not the case. In fact, if an established talking bird is housed with another of the same species, it can encourage its companion to mimic human speech. Its vocabulary will decline, however, if it is not encouraged to express itself in a human voice.

Whether birds can actually comprehend what they repeat is a controversial topic. Certainly, some recent studies have tended to

indicate that parrots may possess some powers of reasoning, notably because of the way they can grasp the meaning of the word 'no'. This, in purely linguistic terms, is a fairly advanced concept, and its use suggests that the bird can comprehend and respond to the situation concerned. Certainly, parrots have a good memory. This may become apparent if they have been mistreated in any way in the past. Often, a reminiscence of a mildly disturbing experience, such as the association of gloves with being caught, will bring forth noisy screeching. Parrots can also remember people, accepting former owners although they may be generally aloof with strangers.

Toys

Most parrots are quite content to sit on the top of their cage, without straying far afield. Nevertheless, there will be times when you will not be able to let the bird out, and for this reason you should provide toys within the cage for all parrots. Unfortunately, plastic articles can be used safely only with budgerigars, and possibly

Below: *Budgerigars are attracted to mirrors, but if a cock bird starts to feed its reflection regularly, remove the mirror for a period.*

Above: *A toy budgerigar can become accepted as a real-life substitute. You can buy many toys for your pet, but avoid cluttering the cage unnecessarily.*

Below: *Out of its cage, your pet budgerigar can still find a suitable perch, in this case conveniently sized toy furniture. A tame budgie will settle regularly on a perch.*

cockatiels, and even then only with care. Not all are of robust construction, and they may conceal sharp projections within, which could cause serious injury. It is safest, therefore, to choose simple toys, such as a mirror fitted onto the side of the cage and a knockabout toy on the floor.

Some budgerigars appreciate ladders, but these take up

Above: *A typical budgerigar cage and accessories. Always consider the ease with which the components, including the cage itself, can be cleaned. Be careful when washing plastic cages as hot water may well cause clear plastic sections to become clouded.*

considerable space in the cage and birds can occasionally become caught up between the rungs. Swings are actually included with some cages, but are rarely used, except by budgerigars. Larger parrots readily destroy the wooden base of the swing, and it is not generally worthwhile to leave such a toy in place in their cages.

Stout metal chains are frequently used to attach bells and other items within a parrot cage. However, always ensure that there is no risk of the bird being caught up in the metal loops. It is also important to consider how easy it will be to clean any toy. Those on the floor of the cage will need to washed quite frequently, for example, so elaborate designs are not recommended. Indeed, for parrots, a piece of wood sliding on a loop of thick wire will usually be much appreciated. It is easy to replace the wood when the original piece has been destroyed.

Behavioural difficulties

One of the most common behavioural problems is seen in cock budgerigars kept on their own with a mirror or toy in their cage, which they come to visualize as a mate. They can become very attached to the object of their

affection, even attempting to mate with it, and will also regurgitate seed in an attempt to feed their reflection or the toy. This behaviour can become pathological, to the extent that the bird concerned starts to lose weight, because of the repeated regurgitation of food. If you become aware of this problem, remove the toy or mirror without delay. The cock bird's ardour will decrease, and later it may even be possible to reinstate the object.

Hen budgerigars housed on their own may occasionally lay eggs on the floor of the cage, becoming very destructive beforehand to any items which can be gnawed, such as sandsheets or cuttlefish bone. The earliest sign that this problem is imminent is the hen sitting in the corner of the cage for most of the day, although she appears well and eats normally. Her droppings are liable to become much bigger immediately before she lays an egg.

Under these circumstances, the best strategy is to leave her undisturbed as far as possible. She may lay several eggs in succession, but should soon tire of them. They will be infertile in any case. Do not remove the eggs as they are laid; this merely encourages repeated laying and will drain the hen's reserves of calcium and the other elements that contribute to the formation of an egg.

In larger parrots, behavioural changes are likely to become apparent when they mature, often from about the age of three years. Behavioural problems may develop, notably displays of aggression under certain circumstances. Apart from carefully introducing a mate, there is little that you can do when faced with this difficulty but wait for the phase to pass. It can bring other difficulties in its wake, however, such as feather plucking, which can be extremely hard to overcome in the long term (see page 56).

Bathing

Birds living indoors are clearly unable to bathe as they would in an aviary, and regular spraying should encourage them to preen normally, reducing the likelihood of feather plucking. Some budgerigars will bathe in a container of water, or roll around on damp greenfood to moisten their feathers, but many of the larger parrots refuse to respond in either way. Lories and mynahs are a notable exception, readily

Below: Spraying will improve the condition of your bird's plumage. Use a clean plant sprayer and aim the nozzle over the cage so that a fine mist falls from above.

immersing themselves in a suitable vessel, as mentioned on page 42.

Most parrots will appreciate a light spray, however, although they may be nervous at first until they are used to it. A clean plant sprayer with a fine nozzle which produces a mist of water droplets is ideal. It is probably best to spray the bird just before you clean out the cage, so that you can change the wet lining immediately afterwards.

Before you begin, remove the food and water pots. Then, with the nozzle directed above the parrot's head and the sprayer held a suitable distance outside the cage, squeeze the handle. Used in this way, the bird will receive a cloud of droplets falling from above rather than being struck directly by a jet of water. Although it may be startled at first, the bird should begin preening shortly afterwards. There is no need to saturate your pet, but a gentle spray two or three times a week will help to improve the condition of the plumage and dampen down the feather dust in the vicinity of the cage. Once the parrot is used to the sprayer, it may well react more positively, holding its wings out to catch the water droplets and showing obvious signs of excitement, such as contracting its pupils and calling out loudly while it is actually being sprayed.

Basic health care

Pet birds are generally very healthy, mainly because they are unlikely to come into contact with the parasites and diseases which affect their counterparts living in the wild. However, their more sedentary lifestyle can bring its own specific problems, such as obesity and boredom. This is particularly likely if the bird is left on its own for long periods confined in a small cage.

Careful management and providing adequate opportunities for exercise can help to prevent these problems arising. Illnesses are most likely to arise soon after you acquire your bird and before it is fully settled in its new surroundings. Diagnosis of avian ailments is often difficult, and you should consult a veterinarian without delay if you suspect your bird is ill. Although treatments such as antibiotics can prove extremely effective, certainly against bacterial infections, it is vital that therapy begins as soon as the signs of illness are apparent. A sick bird declines rapidly, making successful treatment difficult unless medication is given early.

Typical symptoms of an infectious illness will include a decrease in activity and appetite, a change in the appearance of the droppings, and possibly a discharge from the eyes or nostrils. The bird will seem depressed, and may perch with its eyes closed for long periods.

Emergency care

When faced with a sick bird, transfer it to a warm spot, where the temperature averages about 27°C (81°F). This will minimize heat loss from its body. Ensure that food and water are close to the bird, whether or not it is able to perch. Many birds will drink when they are ill, even if they refuse to eat. Medication is often given by this route, although dosing is obviously unreliable under these circumstances. A veterinarian may prefer to administer an antibiotic by means of an injection, or even in a tablet given directly.

Accidents can happen to a bird at any time. It may escape from its cage and fly into a window, stunning itself badly in the process. Under these circumstances, all you can do is transfer it to a box and leave it, hoping that it will recover in these darkened surroundings.

Superficial wounds clot quite readily, but if the end of a claw is broken, for example, the blood loss is likely to be more severe. It is useful to have a styptic pencil to hand for an emergency of this nature, although a cold solution of potash alum (potassium aluminium sulphate), applied on a cotton-wool bud, can prove equally effective.

In general, injuries to birds do not turn septic because of their relatively high body temperature (generally in the region of 41°C/106°F). However, a cat's bite is liable to inject potentially lethal bacteria into a bird's tissues, and should never be neglected, however superficial. Antibiotic treatment is recommended under these circumstances to prevent the development of a generalized infection.

Birds can become caught up, both inside and outside their cage, and it is possible for them to fracture or badly sprain a limb as a result. Seek veterinary advice for accurate diagnosis and treatment. Often, the site of the fracture is towards the top of the leg, which prevents effective splinting. However, the break should repair quite rapidly and the bird will soon show few, if any, adverse effects from its injury.

Claw care

Overgrown claws are one cause of a bird becoming caught up and injuring itself. If you think that the claws of your bird are too long and you are unsure about clipping them, make arrangements for them to be clipped by a veterinarian. Alternatively, this task can be carried out quite easily and safely at home. Restrain the bird in your hand and locate the blood supply, which runs for a short distance down each claw and is visible as a thin pinkish streak in pale claws. Use a sharp pair of bone clippers to nip the overgrown end off. So long as you take care to cut a safe distance

Above: *Clipping the claws of a budgerigar. These often become overgrown, handicapping the bird as it moves around its cage. Use stout claw clippers; not scissors.*

away from the end of the blood supply, this procedure is painless and there is no risk of bleeding.

Scissors are not well suited to the task, since they tend to tear the claw rather than cutting cleanly through it. Although you can obtain tubular sandsheets that fit over the perch to keep the claws in trim by a filing action, these are not very effective. They are also liable to be destroyed by the chewing activities of parrots, including budgerigars, and their rough surfaces can aggravate any foot injuries or pressure points.

Beak trimming

It is well known that caged budgerigars' beaks tend to become overgrown more readily than those

Below: *Overgrown beaks are not uncommon. Here, the top mandible needs to be cut back so that the bird can eat properly.*

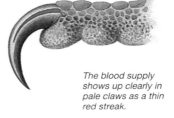

The blood supply shows up clearly in pale claws as a thin red streak.

Clip off the tip of the claw, allowing a generous margin to prevent bleeding.

Above: *It is vital to locate the blood supply before cutting the claw. Then clip carefully as shown, keeping clear of the red streak.*

of aviary birds. This may be partly because aviary birds have more opportunity to exercise their beaks. An overgrown beak needs to be cut back in a similar way to the claws, although it can be harder to locate the blood supply.

Unfortunately, once you start to clip the beak it tends to grow faster, creating a vicious circle. If you are in any doubt, consult your veterinarian for advice and ask him to carry out this task for you. Always compare an overgrown beak with the normal state before deciding to cut it back. It is not a task to be undertaken lightly; if the beak is cut too short, the tip will be sensitive and may

Above: *Feather plucking in a Peach-faced Lovebird. This may reflect a desire to breed, and is often a problem in pet parrots.*

Above: *The use of an Elizabethan collar to prevent feather plucking. A drastic solution, this will also prevent preening while in place.*

cause the bird to stop eating for a period. There is also the risk of blood loss from a beak trimmed too close to the blood supply.

Feather plucking

This condition is poorly understood, although a number of contributory factors can be clearly identified. Once the signs are apparent, little can be done in the way of treatment. Although the feathers may regrow, relapses are not uncommon. Try therefore, to identify the likely causes, and aim to correct these without delay. A poor diet, consisting basically of seed alone,

may underlie some cases. Lack of bathing facilities, boredom and a frustrated desire to breed have been mentioned previously as possible factors causing feather plucking.

Various treatments are available that aim to discourage the bird from pulling its feathers by coating them with a foul-tasting, non-toxic substance. These often prove ineffectual, however, for birds only possess a limited sense of taste and are not so easily deterred. Probably the most effective means of dealing with the problem is to obtain a companion for your bird.

Another kind of feather problem

Below: *Feather cysts are typically associated with Norwich and Gloster Fancy Canaries. They appear as an obvious swelling. A congenital trait that may recur.*

Below: *A tragic case of feather rot, along with feather plucking, in a Lesser Sulphur-crested Cockatoo. There is little that can be done when this stage is reached.*

encountered in canaries – so-called 'feather cysts' – may at first glance appear more akin to a tumour. Feather cysts are a congential weakness; isolated feathers prove too soft to emerge normally and, as a result, curl back beneath the skin, causing the formation of a swelling. In time, the cyst will rupture, shedding its cheesy contents and the affected feathering inside. No treatment is possible. Although the condition sounds most unpleasant, it does not appear to be very distressing for the canary itself, which otherwise lives a normal life.

Other plumage disorders, such as feather rot, French moult and feather lice, are discussed on pages 19 and 20 as points to consider when choosing a pet bird.

Tumours

Other swellings on the body may be more sinister. Tumours are most common in budgerigars, up to one third of these birds being affected by such growths during their lives. Therapy will depend partly on the site of the tumour, and whether or not it is malignant (cancerous).

The benign lumps of fatty tissue described as lipomas are most likely to be encountered in pet birds. Seek veterinary advice if you suspect that your bird could be affected, so that surgery, if considered practical, can be undertaken without delay. Obviously, the earlier the growth is removed, the more likely that surgery will have a successful outcome. Safe anaesthetics are now widely used for birds, but overweight individuals present more of a risk when under an anaesthetic. Recurrences are not uncommon, especially with lipomas, but your budgerigar could live quite happily for a number of years after surgery.

Surgery is not always possible, however, especially in the case of internal tumours, which can be hard to diagnose until they are well advanced. One of the earliest symptoms in budgerigars may be an alteration in cere coloration to almost the 'reverse' of normal. Those of cock birds take on a

brownish cast, whereas those of hens become pale and slightly bluish. An affected budgerigar shows signs of weight loss, becoming 'light' and less active. In the terminal stages in some cases, notably if the kidneys are affected, the bird loses the use of its legs because the tumour compresses and interferes with the nervous supply to the limbs.

There appears to be nothing that you can do to prevent the occurrence of such tumours. Once the bird is showing clear signs of distress, then euthanasia is to be recommended. Although tumours tend to affect birds from middle age onwards, they can occasionally strike budgerigars which are barely mature.

Tumours are not common in other parrots, although the Roseate Cockatoo appears susceptible – like budgerigars – to lipomas. Noticeable growths sometimes affect older parrots; your veterinarian will be able to advise you on the best course of action in an individual case.

Eye infections

The onset of any eye infection can be quite sudden, but early treatment usually leads to an equally rapid recovery. The signs of an eye disorder are unmistakable. The bird will often be reluctant to open the affected eye and the surrounding skin may be swollen. A discharge of tear fluid may also have matted the surrounding plumage, and the bird is likely to rub its head along the perch to relieve irritation.

Treatment is available in the form of an ointment or a liquid. The former option is preferable, since liquid drops may miss their target, whereas a trail of ointment is more visible. Unfortunately, you will need to catch your bird three or four times a day to apply the medication, and it may come to resent this attention. Nevertheless, hold the bird for a few moments afterwards, rather than releasing it straight back into the cage. This will prevent the bird from wiping off the ointment as soon as it is applied, and will give time for it to dissolve at the site of infection.

An eye infection may have arisen from a scratch from a dirty claw, although if both eyes are affected this could well be a symptom of a more generalized infection.

Foot problems

Dirty and hard perches may affect the feet themselves, giving rise to the disease described as bumblefoot, which typically causes swellings to develop on the ball of the foot.

Prevention is straightforward, although occasionally bumblefoot can arise in spite of all precautions, probably because an overgrown claw has penetrated the sole of the foot and left the area open to infection. The bird will be reluctant to use the affected foot. Antibiotic treatment, often in association with surgery at the outset, can prove effective. This should be given before the infection tracks up the leg, or there is a risk that the bacteria may localize around a joint or cause a widespread infection.

Chlamydiosis

Take care when dealing with a sick bird, since some ailments are zoonoses; that is, diseases which can be transmitted to humans. Most notorious of these is undoubtedly psittacosis, now more accurately described as chlamydiosis. The infectious organism, *Chlamydia psittaci* (with features seen in both bacteria and viruses), has been identified in many species, both avian and mammalian, rather than solely in psittacines (the parrots).

Indeed, many human cases show no contact with birds. The incidence of the infection in humans is quite low, with approximately 46 cases being diagnosed annually in the whole of the United States. Typical symptoms are indicative of a serious respiratory disease, and may include pneumonia. If you or a member of your family falls ill, and you suspect that they could be suffering from chlamydiosis, inform the doctor without delay. Antibiotic therapy is effective in most cases.

In birds, bloodstained diarrhoea, runny eyes and nostrils, coupled with severe lethargy can indicate chlamydiosis. Recently imported stock presents perhaps the highest risk, although routine prophylactic medication given during the quarantine period will largely eradicate this threat. (This is used routinely in the USA.) Indeed, since 10 percent of respiratory infections in household cats can entail the

Below: *Symptoms of bumblefoot on a mynah bird. This can be caused by hard, unsuitable perches coupled with a dirty cage.*

Below: *Careful cleaning and treatment can overcome foot infections of this type before they spread further up the legs.*

Above: *A bad case of scaly face caused by mites that bore into the tissue on and around the beak. This infection is easy to treat. Such mites can also affect the legs.*

involvement of the *Chlamydia* organism, other sources of infection can be present in the household.

Parasites
Parasites are rarely encountered in solitary pet birds, although the symptoms of scaly face mites may become apparent even in a budgerigar that has been living on its own for several years. The life cycle of these microscopic mites is unknown, but it is clear that they can exist without giving rise to symptoms. If the typical snail-like tracks become visible on the beak, start treatment without delay, before the more advanced coral-like encrustations develop. Proprietary remedies are available from most pet stores. Alternatively, you can simply dab the affected areas with petroleum jelly, which also serves to suffocate the mites.

Some owners like to treat a newly acquired pet immediately, to ensure that it is not carrying a burden of external parasites. Treatment is easy using a specific aerosol preparation marketed for this purpose and available from pet stores. Follow the directions closely and repeat the treatment as

indicated to ensure the elimination of such parasites.

Internal parasites, notably worms and unicellular organisms known as protozoa, are not usually of any concern to the owner of a pet bird, although in a few cases they can be a source of problems. Seek veterinary advice if signs such as persistent diarrhoea are apparent.

Under normal circumstances, you are unlikely to encounter any problems, and you should be able to enjoy the company of your pet bird without serious worries.

Below: *Sick birds, especially parrots, should be treated with care. This bird is clearly unwell, and needs veterinary treatment.*

The second part of the book will help to guide you in the selection of a particular bird, and covers all the popular species likely to be kept in the home. Availability can vary, however, depending upon where you live, since certain birds and varieties are more common in some countries than in others. The mutations and colour forms are no more difficult to keep than their normal counterparts.

Not everyone looks for the same qualities when choosing a pet bird. In order to help you make a decision, this section considers the size, diet, pet appeal, care and breeding of each species, plus any potential problems you may encounter. An increasingly important consideration in choosing a pet bird is the cost involved, not only of the bird itself but also in its upkeep. Indeed, such is the cost of some of the larger parrots that various insurance schemes are now available to protect you against veterinary costs, and even the loss of your bird. Think carefully before deciding upon a policy of this

type; although the idea may appeal to you, the premiums for such insurance are rather high. Although veterinary costs should be significantly less than for other pets, such as dogs or cats, simple health insurance alone may be worthwhile.

The cost of acquiring larger parrots has risen considerably over recent years, and thefts of such pets have regrettably become more commonplace. Ringing the larger parrots is certainly not recommended, and in any event, rings can be removed to confuse the identity of a particular bird. Tattooing parrots for security reasons is becoming increasingly common and some veterinarians offer this service. The bird is first anaesthetized and usually tattooed under the wing. The safest method, however, is to note any distinguishing marks, photograph your bird and teach it your address or telephone number. It should then be possible to prove beyond reasonable doubt, in court if necessary, that the bird is yours.

Budgerigar

Melopsittacus undulatus

● **Distribution:** Ranges over much of Australia, except the eastern coastal areas and Tasmania. Nomadic by nature.

● **Size:** 18cm (7in).

● **Diet:** A mixture of plain canary seed and millets, including millet sprays. Also greenstuff, carrot and sweet apple.

● **Immatures:** May show a barring pattern on the head down to the cere. The beaks of newly fledged birds may show traces of dark coloration. The eyes are solid, lacking the white irises associated with most adults.

● **Sexing:** Young cock birds have more prominent and purplish ceres than hens. In adult hens, the cere becomes brownish.

● **Pet appeal:** Inexpensive, widely available, easy to care for. Tames readily and can prove a talented talker. Many attractive colours.

The Budgerigar is probably the most popular bird worldwide. It is available in a wide range of colours and crested forms have also been developed. Yet it was only in 1840 that the first living examples were seen outside Australia, when the naturalist John Gould brought them to England. Within fifty years, huge commercial breeding units were established, producing thousands of these parakeets for petseekers. By the early 1870s the first of the colour mutations started to emerge, although there had already been reports of such birds in wild flocks.

Colour forms and mutations
Yellows were among the earliest colours to be seen. Today the most common of the yellow forms

Below: **Lutino Budgerigars**
A pair of birds (cock at top) sharing the deep overall yellow and white facial markings typical of this form.

Above: Albino Budgerigar
In this colour variety, the plumage is pure white and (as in Lutinos) the eyes are red. This is a cock.

available is the Lutino, recognizable by its red eyes. In cock birds, the cere remains purplish throughout their lives, rather than turning blue, as is more usual. The same applies to the Albino, a pure white form of the Budgerigar, again with red eyes.

The first of the blue varieties was reported at the end of the 1870s, when the Sky Blue mutation emerged. Subsequently, the superimposition of the so-called 'dark factor' gave rise to the Cobalt and Mauve forms. In green series budgerigars, the natural light green coloration has been altered by the addition of one or two dark factors to their genetic make-up, to produce Dark Green and Olive Green respectively.

The violet factor, which emerged during the 1930s, has a similar effect. Although it may be present in green series birds, it is only when combined with the dark and blue characters that the violet factor gives rise to the so-called visual violet budgerigars.

At about the same time, the coloration and markings of the budgerigar were radically modified with the appearance of the pied

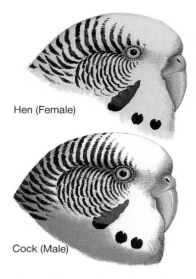

Hen (Female)

Cock (Male)

Above: The cere above the beak provides a useful key to sexing budgerigars. It is brown in a mature hen and bluish in most cock birds.

Above: **Cobalt Budgerigar**
This colour shows the effect of the dark factor on the Sky Blue.

Below: **Grey Budgerigar**
From Australian stock, the Grey is seen in shades from light to dark.

Above: **Dark Green Budgerigar**
*This colour is deeper than the
natural colour of wild budgerigars
because of the influence of one
so-called 'dark factor' in its genetic
make up. The Dark Green
mutation, also seen in wild flocks,
was one of the earliest colour
forms to become established.*

mutations. These can be
distinguished on genetic grounds,
but basically the Recessive form, of
Scandinavian origin, is smaller than
its Dominant counterpart, which
first appeared in Australia. In
addition, Recessive Pieds have
solid plum-coloured eyes even
when adult, whereas Dominant

65

Pieds have black pupils and white irises. Blue of any shade, including violet, can be combined with areas of white plumage, and the traditional darker head and wing markings may also be broken or virtually absent. Today, green and yellow pieds are equally common. Other colours,

Left: **Full Circular Crested**
A Grey Budgerigar with a complete fringe of feathers around the head.

Below:
Dominant Pied Budgerigars
These are the most common colour combinations. Note the characteristic white irises.

changed to brown. The most recent Budgerigar mutation – the Spangled – which appeared during 1978 in Australia, is also of this type. Here, the feathers on the back resemble those of a Pearl Cockatiel, i.e. with dark edges and light centres.

A separate branch of the Budgerigar Fancy has concentrated on the development of the three crested mutations. The full-circular variant is probably the most striking, resembling the crest of a Gloster Corona Canary (see page 106). In the Half-circular, the crest is restricted to a fringe over the front of the head. The Tufted mutation has a raised crest of plumage and, like the other mutations, this feature can be combined with any of the colours or colour variants. If these birds appeal

Above: **Recessive Pied**
A hen bird with typical deep plum eyes which lack white irises.

such as grey – which also exists as a pure mutation – may feature on pieds, in this case on a white background.

The Opaline mutation has resulted in changes to the pattern of markings on the head and wings. The head markings are lightened and a clear area at the top of the wings should form the characteristic 'V' shape, which is a feature of a good exhibition Opaline. This characteristic can be transferred irrespective of colour, so that other colours, such as Opaline Violets, can be bred.

There have also been modifications to the coloration of the wings. Yellow-wings have a body coloration of green, and Whitewings are blue. In the Cinnamon, the markings are

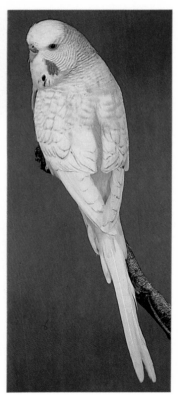

Above: **Spangled Sky Blue**
The white feathers have pale centres and dark edges.

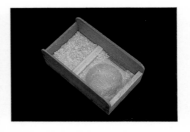

Above: *A typical budgerigar nesting box showing the 'concave' (usually covered with shavings) where the hen bird lays her eggs.*

Top left: *A 4-week-old budgerigar. The barring on the forehead is a typical sign of immaturity.*

Left: **Tufted Budgerigar**
Here, the feathers on the forehead are raised in a tuft above the cere. Tufted birds can be any colour.

to you, it may be necessary to find a specialist breeder. Although these mutations have been known for several decades, they are still not widely seen.

Buying a pet budgerigar
It should not be difficult to obtain a young budgerigar as a pet if you are not especially concerned about acquiring a particular variety. Budgerigars are generally inexpensive, although some colours or colour combinations are more costly than others, and exhibition birds can fetch large sums of money compared to 'pet' birds.

Obtain a young bird about six weeks old, following the guidelines suggested at the beginning of this section. The depth of coloration is unlikely to alter significantly as your pet matures, although its throat spots will probably become larger when it moults into adult plumage. The barring on the head, if present, will recede. The irises will start to appear in the eyes from about three months onwards and the cere will alter in coloration, depending on the variety concerned.

The lifespan of budgerigars can be very variable. Seven or eight years is an average figure, but

Above: *An overhead view of a budgerigar nestbox with both parent birds attending the young and eggs. Budgerigars will breed prolifically, laying a clutch of four to six eggs. It is common practice to move eggs or chicks between nestboxes to 'even up' the ages.*

individuals living well into their teens, and occasionally into their twenties, are not unknown. Budgerigars are particularly suitable as pets for children; they are not aggressive and are unlikely to bite a finger that is carelessly inserted into the cage.

If you want to breed a pair of budgerigars, keep them in a breeding cage with a nestbox attached. A wooden concave on the floor of the nestbox serves as a base for the eggs. The average clutch consists of four to six eggs, laid on alternate days. These should hatch after an incubation period of 18 days, and the young birds fledge at about five weeks. By this stage, the hen is likely to be incubating a second clutch of eggs. For successful breeding, it may be best to keep two pairs of budgerigars in adjoining cages since the sound of their companions seems to encourage breeding behaviour. Two budgerigars are often more reluctant to nest than two pairs housed close together.

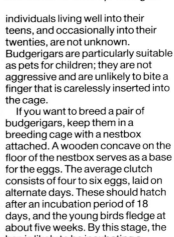

Left: *Baby budgerigars are ideal for taming as pet birds. Their lively and friendly natures have endeared them to literally millions of people.*

69

Cockatiel

Nymphicus hollandicus
- **Distribution:** Over most of Australia, apart from the coastal areas, and especially on the eastern side of the country. Absent from Tasmania.
- **Size:** 30cm (12in).
- **Diet:** A mixture of cereal seeds, notably plain canary seeds and millet, with sunflower, hemp and safflower. Also provide greenstuff, carrot and fruit.
- **Immatures:** Resemble adult hens, but the cere is usually pink rather than grey and the tail is shorter.
- **Sexing:** Hens have greyish facial coloration and barred tails.
- **Pet appeal:** Bears a striking resemblance to cockatoos, but is more manageable, especially for the novice pet bird owner.

Although not as well known as the Budgerigar, the Cockatiel is becoming increasingly popular as a pet. Cockatiels have been kept in aviaries for many years and were first seen in Europe at about the same time as the Budgerigar. Yet mutations did not occur until the 1940s, when the Pied form first emerged in the United States. As with the Budgerigar, the pied markings are very variable, and some birds may show only slight areas of white against their predominantly grey plumage.

The most striking of the Cockatiel mutations is undoubtedly the Lutino, which for some time was

Below: **Normal Cockatiels**
A fine pair, with the male at left clearly distinguishable by its yellow face. Cockatiels make easy pets.

Above: **Lutino Cockatiel**
In this popular colour form, the grey plumage of the normal is changed to a creamy yellow – a splendid foil for the cheeks.

also known as the Albino or White. This is strictly incorrect, since the Lutino has yellow plumage and retains the orange cheek patches. The genuine Albino cockatiel – pure white with red eyes – is scarce at present. Although cock grey cockatiels can be easily sexed by their yellow heads, this distinction is not apparent in the Lutino. Here, the barring on the tail provides a means of distinguishing the sexes. This is not as clear a distinction as in normals, but on close examination Lutino cocks can be recognized by their pure yellow tails, with no trace of the darker barring apparent on the hens.

The Cinnamon, a mutation in which the body is an attractive shade of milk chocolate, can be sexed in the same way as normal Greys. Although the body colour in Cinnamons can vary in depth, these cockatiels do not undergo the dramatic change in colour which occurs in males of another mutation – Pearl cockatiels – when they attain

Above:
Pearl Cinnamon (l)/Pied (r)
These attractive forms show how changes in colour and markings can be achieved by breeding.

sexual maturity. Normally the pearl markings create plumage with a light centre and dark borders. In adult cocks, however, the hormonal influence causes these lighter areas to be obscured by the deposition of the dark pigment melanin. As a result, such birds are usually indistinguishable from the Grey, except sometimes in the shoulder region, where traces of the lighter pearl markings may still be seen.

As with the Budgerigar, it has proved possible to combine changes in colour of cockatiels with modifications to the markings, giving rise to striking varieties such as Pearl Cinnamons.

The majority of the mutations, including the Lutino, are available at low cost. The greatest number of birds is seen at the end of the summer. Over the winter months, however, it may be more difficult to obtain a genuine young cockatiel, since these birds are usually bred in outside aviaries rather than in cages.

Cockatiels are usually independent of their parents by about seven weeks and, although they may be rather nervous at first, they should soon settle down in the home to become devoted pets.

Peach-faced Lovebird

Agapornis roseicollis
● **Distribution:** Southwestern Africa.
● **Size:** 15cm (6in).
● **Diet:** A mixture of cereal seeds, plus sunflower and safflower. Also offer greenfood and fruit.
● **Immatures:** Usually duller overall, with dark markings on the beak.
● **Sexing:** There are no reliable visual distinctions between the sexes.
● **Pet appeal:** Easy to accommodate, lively and easy to tame. Superbly decorative.

The Peach-faced is the best known member of this group of small African parrots, and a number of mutations and varieties are also becoming well established. There is a striking Lutino form, for example, which retains the pinkish facial markings of the normal combined with a pure yellow body coloration, creating an attractive contrast. Another mutation, corresponding to that of the Budgerigar, is the 'dark factor' which, as its name suggests, deepens the coloration in green and greenish blue birds.

As yet, no pure blue mutation has arisen in the Peach-faced Lovebird. All 'blues' have a greenish tinge to their plumage and retain a trace of the pinkish facial coloration, which would be absent in a genuine blue mutation. This also means that instead of a corresponding pied variety of blue and white, the pied is a combination of greenish blue and pale yellow. There is no albino either, but the counterpart in this instance is known as the Cremino, which has an attractive lemon body coloration offset by a pale pinkish face (i.e. paler than the Lutino).

The naming of Peach-faced Lovebird colours can be confusing, since several names are often applied to the same mutation. Probably the most widely used term for the bluish form is Pastel Blue, although individuals of a predominantly blue shade are also described as White-faced Blues. The yellow form of the Peach-faced Lovebird is less widely available than its blue relative, and is often

Below: Peach-faced Lovebird
The normal colour form. The facial coloration develops to its fullest intensity as the bird matures.

referred to by its traditional name of 'Golden Cherry' rather than Yellow or Dilute. Its dark rather than reddish eyes distinguish it from the Lutino. When the Yellow is combined with the Pastel Blue, the form known as the 'Silver Cherry' or White is produced, which is silverish white overall. Other colours also exist, including a Cinnamon variant.

Unfortunately, in spite of their name, lovebirds will not take readily to the introduction of a companion to their cage, unlike budgerigars or cockatiels. It is possible for a pair to breed successfully in the home, but you cannot distinguish pairs reliably by any plumage differences.

Unlike most parrots, lovebirds construct a nest within their nesting chamber. They may employ an unusual method of carrying suitable material to their nest; feathers and bark stripped off branches are tucked carefully in among the plumage of the rump, rather than carried in the beak. The incubation period is about 23 days and the young lovebirds hatch in a covering of red down.

The best time to obtain a young Peach-faced Lovebird is when it has left the nest and has started to eat independently, at about six or seven weeks of age.

Above:
Cremino Peach-faced Lovebird
In this form, the body is an elegant lemon yellow; the pinkish face of the normal is still apparent.

Below: **Pastel Blue**
This attractive variation is also known as the 'White-faced Blue'.

Masked Lovebird
Agapornis personata
- **Distribution:** Northeastern Tanzania.
- **Size:** 14cm (5.5in).
- **Diet:** A mixture of cereal seeds, plus sunflower and safflower, with some greenfood and fruit.
- **Immatures:** Duller, with black markings on the beak.
- **Sexing:** No reliable visual distinctions between the sexes.
- **Pet appeal:** Attractive and not noisy. Distinctive coloration.

This species is seen less often than the Peach-faced and fewer colour forms are established. The oldest of the lovebird colours is the Blue mutation, whose ancestry dates back to the 1920s. This form was established using wild mutant stock, and although sometimes described as the Blue Masked, the colour of the mask remains black, whereas the green body coloration is altered to blue.

There is also a dilute version of the normal Masked, which is known as the 'yellow'. In these birds, the distribution of colour is not affected, only its density, creating birds of lighter colour overall.

The so-called White Masked has a combination of white and blue plumage, corresponding to the yellow and green areas respectively seen in the normal. The mask is paler than normal.

Below: **Masked Lovebirds**
In these lovebirds, the white eye rings show up very clearly against the dark 'mask' of the head.

Above: **Blue Masked Lovebird**
*Here, the black mask remains but
the green plumage of the normal
form is transformed to subtle blue.*

Below: **Yellow Masked Lovebird**
*The 'diluting' effect of this
mutation causes all the colours to
be paler. The mask is less distinct.*

Fischer's Lovebird

Agapornis fischeri

- **Distribution:** Northern Tanzania.
- **Size:** 14cm (5.5in).
- **Diet:** A mixture of cereal seeds, plus sunflower and safflower, with some greenfood and fruit.
- **Immatures:** Duller, with black markings on the beak.
- **Sexing:** No reliable visual distinctions between the sexes.
- **Pet appeal:** Attractive and easy to accommodate in the home.

Fischer's Lovebird is considered to be closely related to the Masked, as both belong to the so-called 'white-eye ring' group – from the fleshy white circles around the eyes. However, mutations of Fischer's Lovebird are not yet as common as they are in the Peach-faced and Masked.

Feather plucking in this species is usually a reflection of a desire to nest and, whenever given the opportunity, lovebirds will roost in a nestbox. It is possible to breed Fischer's Lovebirds in the home if they are provided with adequate seclusion and a suitable nestbox. This should have internal dimensions of about 23cm (9in) in all directions. The only problem with breeding lovebirds indoors is that hatchability may be disappointing. The reason for this is unclear, but it may be due to low humidity. Fischer's usually make good parents and rearing the chicks should be straightforward, provided the nest is left undisturbed during this time.

Lovebirds can live for 15 years or even longer, although it may be difficult to determine the age – and therefore life expectancy as a pet – of imported adult birds. Adult Fischer's, as with all lovebirds, may prove rather nervous. It is best to obtain young birds as pets.

Below: **Fischer's Lovebird**
Splendid colour and a willingness to settle down in the home make these birds an ideal pet choice.

...most of central
...road belt from the
...slands in the west across to
...nwest Tanzania and Kenya.
● **Size:** 33cm (13in).
● **Diet:** Parrot food, nuts, fruit and greenstuff.
● **Immatures:** Recognizable by their dark irises, whereas those of adults are bright yellow.
● **Sexing:** Cocks usually have darker wings, but this is not entirely reliable since some regional differences do occur.
● **Pet appeal:** Probably the best talking parrot.

The Grey Parrot is highly valued as a pet and today it is much easier to obtain a genuinely tame bird because many more are hand reared. Youngsters are very demanding, and you should only contemplate obtaining one of these parrots if you are able to devote considerable time and attention to it. In return, you should have a lifelong companion, since Grey Parrots will live for decades.

Mature Grey Parrots are nervous by nature, and will not settle well in domestic surroundings. Untame adult birds frequently hiss when approached at close quarters, and thus are often described as 'growlers'.

Grey Parrots are not especially noisy birds, however, certainly when compared with New World species, such as Amazons (see pages 82-86). They learn to whistle easily – sounds of this type being akin to those of their natural calls – and can develop a large vocabulary. Grey Parrots may be reluctant to talk with a stranger nearby, however; only when they no longer feel threatened will they speak, as they are naturally shy. In this respect, Grey Parrots are totally different from mynah birds, who seem to delight in being the centre of attention.

In spite of their broad distribution in the wild, there is little recognized variation in the appearance of these parrots. Indeed, the Timneh

subspecies (*P.e.timneh*), is the only distinctive form recognized in mainland Africa. It occurs in the western part of the range and can be distinguished immediately by its maroon (rather than red) tail. Its grey plumage is also significantly darker than normal. Conversely, lighter coloured Grey Parrots, sometimes described as 'Silvers' are found further eastwards. These tend to be more expensive. They are not recognized as a subspecies. All forms of the Grey appear equally talented as mimics.

An unusual but insignificant plumage variant is the presence of scattered red feathers over the body. This feature is variable and may not be apparent after the next moult. It may reflect a nutritional deficiency, although some people claim that this aberration is more likely to be a sign of old age.

The intelligent and sensitive natures of Grey Parrots make them susceptible to the vice of feather plucking, which can rapidly become an habitual problem. (See page 19 for more on feather plucking.)

Unfortunately, it is not possible to sex Grey Parrots reliably by visual means, but surgical sexing is now widely used to identify pairs for breeding purposes. Hen Greys kept on their own may occasionally lay a clutch of (infertile) eggs, often with little prior warning. If you obtain a mate, it may be possible to breed these parrots successfully in the home. They do not require spacious surroundings for this purpose. Serious nesting attempts are unlikely to be made until the birds are about four years old. The incubation period is approximately four weeks and, if all goes well, the young Greys should fledge when three months old. Their eye coloration begins to alter and lighten from about six months onwards. Be prepared for disappointment, however, since not all pairs prove reliable parents. Leave them alone as much as possible and offer a varied diet to ensure the maximum chance of success.

When breeding, tame individuals may become aggressive.

Above: **Grey Parrot**
*One of the most familiar pet
parrots. It will reward attention with*
*intelligent and faithful devotion. An
excellent talker that will also
readily mimic household sounds.*

Senegal Parrot

Poicephalus senegalus
● **Distribution:** Ranges over the African countryside from Senegal east to Chad.
● **Size:** 23cm (9in).
● **Diet:** Parrot food, fruit and greenstuff.
● **Immatures:** Characterized by their dark irises.
● **Sexing:** There are no reliable distinguishing features between the sexes.
● **Pet appeal:** Colourful and can become tame. Their small size makes them easy to cater for in the home.

Senegals are similar to the Grey Parrot in terms of temperament. If obtained when young, they can make great companions, but older birds will not settle well and remain nervous. Look carefully for Senegals with blackish eyes, therefore, to show they are young; those with yellow irises are adults.

Like related species, these parrots are especially keen on peanuts, and in the wild they will raid native villages to obtain them. None of the *Poicephalus* parrots are especially noisy, and their calls – a series of rasping whistles – are not disturbing either.

There are another eight species in this genus, some of which are occasionally seen. These include the Meyer's Parrot (*P.meyeri*), which is found across much of southern Africa and is quite variable in coloration. Indeed, the yellow underparts of the Senegal can vary in depth of colour from yellow through orange to red. This can give rise to confusion with the Red-bellied Parrot (*P.rufiventris*), but this species has brown rather than green wings as a distinguishing feature.

Below: **Senegal Parrots**
These compact brightly coloured parrots can become rewarding pets, if obtained when young.

Poicephalus parrots have occasionally been bred successfully in the home. They need a stout nestbox, since they can prove quite destructive at this time. Up to four eggs form the usual clutch and these should hatch after an incubation period of 28 days. The young birds will fledge when they are about nine weeks old.

Above: **Red-bellied Parrots**
These delicately hued parrots from eastern Africa are similar in size and temperament to Senegals. In this pair, the male is at right.

Below: **Meyer's Parrots**
This is yet another of the several striking species of Poicephalus *parrots that may be available.*

Orange-winged Amazon

Amazona amazonica

● **Distribution:** Over much of northern South America, including the islands of Trinidad and Tobago.

● **Size:** 30cm (12in).

● **Diet:** A parrot mixture, supplemented with daily supplies of fruit, greenstuff and vegetables such as carrot.

● **Immatures:** Similar to adults, but with dark eyes.

● **Sexing:** No visible distinction between the sexes.

● **Pet appeal:** Tames quite readily and proves a talented mimic.

The Amazons are a group of 27 species of parrots found exclusively in the Americas. They are often described as 'Green Parrots', simply because this colour tends to predominate in the plumage of many species. The Orange-winged is commonly kept as a pet but, like other members of this genus, can prove noisy in the home.

Below: **Orange-winged Amazon**
These common parrots are widely available as pet birds. They are noisy, however, and do need plenty of space for exercise.

Blue-fronted Amazon
Amazona aestiva
● **Distribution:** Bolivia, Brazil, Paraguay and northern Argentina.
● **Size:** 35cm (14in).
● **Diet:** A parrot mixture, with fruit, greenstuff and similar items on a daily basis.
● **Immatures:** Similar to adults, but with dark eyes and duller overall.
● **Sexing:** No visible distinction between the sexes.
● **Pet appeal:** Attractive and responsive to training.

The Blue-fronted Amazon is similar to the Orange-winged, but is larger overall. In addition, the red markings on the wings and tail are more intense than those of the Orange-winged Amazon. The beak coloration of the Blue-front is also

Above: **Blue-fronted Amazon**
A long-lived and trainable parrot for the home. It is noticeably larger than the Orange-winged Amazon.

darker, being dark grey to black, while Orange-wings tend to have horn-coloured beaks.

Pairs of Blue-fronted Amazons have nested successfully in the home on several occasions. The incubation period is about 29 days and the young parrots leave the nest after about nine weeks. However, when they are in breeding condition these parrots can change their character quite noticeably and may become aggressive towards their owner during this period.

Reliable records show that Blue-fronted Amazons can live for nearly a century in ideal captive conditions.

Mealy Amazon

Amazona farinosa

● **Distribution:** Southern Mexico to northern South America, and as far south as Bolivia and Brazil, south of the Amazon.

● **Size:** 38cm (15in).

● **Diet:** Parrot mixture with fruit, greenstuff and vegetables such as carrot.

● **Immatures:** Reduced yellow markings on the head and dark irises.

● **Sexing:** No visible distinction between the sexes.

● **Pet appeal:** An imposing species that can become very tame.

Various distinctive races of the Mealy Amazon are recognized, some of which are much more colourful than others. The Blue-crowned (*A.f. guatemalae*), from the northern part of the range, is especially striking, with bluish coloration clearly visible on its head.

The Mealy Amazon is probably the noisiest member of its group; its powerful, far-carrying call is typically heard morning and evening. There is no point in scolding your bird if it does call repeatedly. Simply cover the cage with its usual cover and the parrot will become quiet when confronted with sudden darkness. Remove the cover after a short period and use this technique to train the parrot not to screech repeatedly. Never use a woollen cover, though, since your bird may become caught up in the material if it attempts to hold on to the sides of the cage. These larger parrots can become quite possessive towards their owners and may call simply to attract attention to themselves.

Below: **Mealy Amazon**
Although large and noisy, the Mealy Amazon can become a gratifying if rather possessive pet.

White-fronted Amazon
Amazona albifrons
● **Distribution:** Central America, from Mexico to Costa Rica.
● **Size:** 25cm (10in).
● **Diet:** Parrot mixture, fruit and nuts, greenstuff and carrot.
● **Immatures:** A yellowish tinge to the white plumage above the beak and less red apparent on the sides of the face than in adults.
● **Sexing:** Cock birds have red wing coverts (plumage at the edges of the wing).
● **Pet appeal:** Easier to cater for and less raucous than the larger Amazons featured here.

These small birds are quite straightforward to look after in

Above: **White-fronted Amazon**
A relatively small and easily maintained Amazon parrot. This is a female, as shown by the green (rather than red) wing coverts.

domestic surroundings and are easier to handle than their bigger relatives. As pets kept on their own, White-fronted Amazons can prove talented mimics.

The White-fronted Amazon is the only species that can be sexed easily. It may be possible to breed them if they are housed in a flight cage equipped with a nestbox. Three or four eggs can be anticipated and these take about a month to hatch, with the chicks fledging about two months later.

85

Yellow-fronted Amazon

Amazona ochrocephala
● **Distribution:** From Mexico southwards to Peru and eastwards to the Guianas and Venezuela.
● **Size:** 35cm (14in).
● **Diet:** Parrot mixture, plus fruit and greenstuff.
● **Immatures:** Dark irises.
● **Sexing:** No visible distinction.
● **Pet appeal:** Tames quite readily and talks well.

Up to nine distinct races of the Yellow-fronted Amazon are recognized and they tend to be localized in their distribution. Essentially, they differ in the relative proportions of yellow present on the head. The Yellow-naped subspecies (*A.o. auropalliata*), for example, has just a thin band of yellow across the back of its neck. In contrast, the Double Yellow-headed (*A.o. oratrix*) has a completely yellow head, although this feature is not apparent in young birds at first. The Yellow-fronted Amazon (*A.o. ochrocephala*) from northern South America is the race most commonly encountered. Here, the yellow feathering is confined to the area of the head that extends back from the cere above the eyes.

Above: **Double Yellow-head**
As the common name implies, in this race the yellow coloration extends over the entire head.

Below: **Yellow-fronted Amazon**
In this, the most commonly seen race of the group, the yellow is limited to a patch above the cere.

Maximilian's Parrot

Pionus maximiliana

● **Distribution:** Much of eastern South America, extending from northern Brazil to Bolivia, Paraguay and Argentina.
● **Size:** 30cm (12in).
● **Diet:** Parrot food, plus fruit and greenstuff.

Above: **Blue-headed Parrot**
Stunning colour and an ability to tame well when hand reared.

Above: **Maximilian's Parrot**
A good choice for a pet parrot, although not as colourful nor widely known as some parrots.

● **Immatures:** Duller, often with reddish foreheads and less blue on the breast than adults.
● **Sexing:** No visual distinction between the sexes.
● **Pet appeal:** Tolerant and tames easily. Deserves wider appreciation.

When obtained young, these parrots can become very tame and prove quite capable mimics. Adult birds sometimes wheeze rather disconcertingly, however, and this noise may also indicate the fungal disease aspergillosis, to which *Pionus* parrots appear susceptible.

The *Pionus* parrots as a group are not brightly coloured, and Maximilian's Parrot is no exception. The only other *Pionus* species found with any degree of regularity is the Blue-headed Parrot (*P.menstruus*). It is more striking than Maximilian's Parrot, having a deep blue head. In young birds this feature is not usually pronounced, although they can also be distinguished at this stage by the presence of a red frontal band above the beak.

Blue and Gold Macaw

Ara ararauna

● **Distribution:** From Panama (in Central America) southwards into South America, extending to Bolivia, Paraguay and Brazil.

● **Size:** 86cm (34in).

● **Diet:** Parrot food with fruit, vegetables and greenstuff. Also appreciates nuts, such as brazils, when available.

● **Immatures:** Characterized by their dark eyes.

● **Sexing:** No clear visual distinction between the sexes, although hens usually have smaller heads.

● **Pet appeal:** Loyal and gentle to their owners.

These large striking parrots can become great companions, but they are not particularly talented as talking birds. Unfortunately, their large size makes housing them indoors rather difficult, and their powerful beaks will soon find any weakness in the design and construction of their quarters.

If you are not accustomed to dealing with parrotlike birds, the considerable power of their beaks may cause handling problems.

Macaws generally breed quite readily, so it should not be difficult to obtain one of these majestic birds if you can provide the necessary facilities to house them.

Below: **Blue and Gold Macaw**
These magnificent parrots cannot be recommended for beginners or small homes. Given space, they can become lifelong companions.

Green-winged Macaw
Ara chloroptera
● **Distribution:** Eastern Panama (in Central America) southwards over much of northern South America to Bolivia, Paraguay and northern Argentina.
● **Size:** 90cm (36in).
● **Diet:** Parrot food with fruit and greenstuff. Offer nuts, such as brazils, when available.
● **Immatures:** Characterized by their dark eyes.
● **Sexing:** No clear distinction between the sexes, although hens usually have smaller heads.
● **Pet appeal:** Spectacular and striking. Will tame readily if obtained when young.

These macaws are just as demanding as the Blue and Gold and possess a similarly loud call. However, they can become very tame in domestic surroundings.

Above: **Green-winged Macaw**
Although large and powerful, these macaws have nested successfully in fairly compact indoor conditions.

Like some Amazons, all macaws have a strong musky body odour and this species is no exception. The scent may be produced from the preen gland located above the base of the tail.

When excited, the bare facial area of these macaws becomes reddened, as blood flow to the skin increases. Macaws can use their large bills to devastating effect on woodwork, so always ensure that you have an adequate supply of suitable branches available to distract them.

The third member of the multicoloured macaw group is the Scarlet, also known as the Red and Yellow (*A. macao*). It requires similar care to the Green-winged Macaw.

89

Red-shouldered Macaw

Ara nobilis
● **Distribution:** Venezuela and the Guianas southwards into Brazil.
● **Size:** 30cm (12in).
● **Diet:** Parrot food and smaller cereal seeds, plus fruit and greenstuff.
● **Immatures:** Have dark irises, no blue area above the beak and lack the red feathering along the edge of the wing.
● **Sexing:** No clear visible means of distinguishing between the sexes.
● **Pet appeal:** Typical macaw appearance, but much easier to accommodate than related species.

This is the smallest member of the macaw group. It is one of a number of predominantly green species, sometimes decribed collectively as the dwarf macaws. If obtained when young, they can become just as tame as their larger counterparts.

This species is often divided into two subspecies. Hahn's Macaw (*A.n. nobilis*), found in the northern part of the range, has a dark grey beak which distinguishes it from the Noble Macaw (*A.n. cumanensis*) found further south. In the Noble Macaw, the beak is much paler, with a horn-coloured upper mandible and a grey lower portion. It is often slightly larger than Hahn's Macaw. It is quite scarce in avicultural collections and less likely to be seen than its more northerly relative.

Pairs will nest quite satisfactorily indoors, laying up to four eggs, which should start to hatch after an incubation period of about 25 days. The young chicks will leave the nest when they are approximately two months old and should be able to feed themselves shortly afterwards.

Right: **Hahn's Macaw**
This northern subspecies is the most widely seen form of the Red-shouldered Macaw.

Red-masked Conure

Aratinga erythrogenys
● **Distribution:** Ecuador and Peru.
● **Size:** 33cm (13in).
● **Diet:** Parrot mixture with cereal seeds, plus fruit and greenstuff.
● **Immatures:** No red plumage on the head or thighs.
● **Sexing:** No reliable visual means of distinguishing the sexes.
● **Pet appeal:** Tames easily, colourful and full of character.

The description 'conure' is applied to certain parakeets from the Americas. The Red-masked is one of a group of conures which, although predominantly green, have red markings as well. The red on the head is most pronounced in the Red-masked. Other species of similar appearance include the Red-fronted (*A. wagleri*), which has an area of red plumage confined to the crown, and the Mitred (*A. mitrata*), with a variable amount of red plumage scattered over its body, noticeably on the forehead.

Conures are generally less expensive to buy than parrots such as Amazons, yet they can become

equally tame. The Red-masked is no exception and young birds can be taught to say a few words.

Above: **Red-masked Conures**
These handsome birds can be boisterous and noisy, but repay attention with loyal affection. Conures in general are becoming more widely kept as pet birds.

Sun Conure

Aratinga solstitialis

● **Distribution:** Guianas to northwestern Brazil.
● **Size:** 30cm (12in).
● **Diet:** Parrot mixture, with smaller cereal seeds, plus fruit and greenstuff.
● **Immatures:** Usually less colourful, often predominantly greenish.
● **Sexing:** No visual distinction possible between the sexes.
● **Pet appeal:** Colourful and lively.

The Sun Conure is an exceptionally beautiful bird but, in common with other *Aratinga* species, it is liable to prove noisy in the home, which can prove a serious drawback. These conures tend to breed quite freely in collections, so that captive-bred stock is usually available.

A 30cm (12in) cube will make a suitable nestbox, and if a pair do breed you can expect up to four eggs in the clutch. They should hatch after about 26 days and the young conures will fledge at about eight weeks.

Sun Conures appear to be more susceptible to the vice of feather plucking than related species. Adult birds may pluck their offspring, especially when they are keen to nest again.

Below: **Sun Conure**
Superb fiery coloration and a lively nature are the main appeal of this attractive conure. It is free-breeding but can be rather noisy.

Maroon-bellied Conure
Pyrrhura frontalis
● **Distribution:** Brazil to Uruguay, Paraguay and Argentina.
● **Size:** 25cm (10in).
● **Diet:** Parrot food, including small pine nuts and cereal seeds such as millets, fruit and greenstuff.
● **Immatures:** Duller overall, with shorter tails.
● **Sexing:** No visual means of distinguishing the sexes.
● **Pet appeal:** Tames very readily.

These conures, sometimes also described as Red-bellied Conures, are much quieter than the *Aratingas*, and are thus more suitable as household pets. They are lively and inquisitive birds that nest very freely,

Above: **Maroon-bellied Conure**
This compact conure has much to commend it as a pet bird, notably its relative quietness compared to the Aratinga *conures. It breeds readily in captivity and tames well.*

making youngsters quite easily obtainable.

Other *Pyrrhura* species are relatively scarce in aviculture, although the similar Green-cheeked Conure (*P.molinae*) is now quite well established. It resembles the Maroon-bellied in appearance, but can be easily distinguished by the reddish upper surface of its tail feathers. Those of the Maroon-bellied are predominantly green, with red confined just to the tip.

Canary-winged Parakeet

Brotogeris versicolorus

● **Distribution:** Over much of the Amazon drainage basin and further south over a broad area of Brazil, extending to Bolivia, Paraguay and Argentina.

● **Size:** 23cm (9in).

● **Diet:** Typical parrot mix supplemented with the smaller cereal seeds. Offer fruit and greenstuff on a regular basis.

● **Immatures:** Less colourful wing markings.

● **Sexing:** No visual means of distinction possible.

● **Pet appeal:** Hand-reared birds can be very tame.

There are two distinctive subspecies of this parakeet; the White-winged (*B.v. versicolorus*) is olive green, whereas the Canary-winged (*B.v. chiriri*) is a bright grass green with canary-yellow wing markings. A striking blue mutation of this species has occurred, in which sky blue plumage is offset against white wing markings, but it is very scarce at present.

These parakeets can become extraordinarily tame, but may also become rather jealous of other pets. It will be difficult, for example, to integrate a pair successfully if one parakeet is already an established pet in the household.

Canary-winged Parakeets can mimic sounds and the human voice quite successfully, and may even learn to say a few words. These birds are very fond of pieces of banana, which they chew and then scatter around, making the cage rather sticky.

The Orange-flanked or Grey-cheeked Parakeet (*Brotogeris pyrrhopterus*) is also available. It originates from Ecuador and Peru.

Below: **Orange-flanked Parakeet**
The striking orange coloration of this species can be seen more clearly when the wings are lifted.

Ring-necked Parakeet
Psittacula krameri

● **Distribution:** Occurs over a wider area than any other species of psittacine, from northwest Africa through parts of Asia as far east as Burma, and possibly extending into China. It has been introduced successfully to many other localities around the world.

● **Size:** 40.5cm (16in).

● **Diet:** Parrot mixture, with fruit and greenstuff on a regular basis.

● **Immatures:** Resemble the adult hen, but have greyish irises and paler bills.

● **Sexing:** Mature cocks are easily recognizable by their pink neck ring and black facial markings.

● **Pet appeal:** Elegant appearance and may talk quite well.

This species has a long avicultural history, and may have been known to Alexander the Great (356-323 BC). The related, but larger, Alexandrine Parakeet (*P. eupatria*) in fact bears his name. Apart from the variation in size, the only plumage distinction is that Alexandrines also have red shoulder patches. The African race of the Ring-necked (*P.k. krameri*) can be separated from its Indian counterpart (*P.k. manillensis*) by virtue of its beak coloration, with the lower mandible being dull red rather than black.

Among the colour mutations now

Below: **Ring-necked Parakeet**
This is quite clearly a male, with the typical collar of pink feathers and the black facial markings.

95

Above: **Ring-necked Parakeets**
The larger photograph shows a female of the Cinnamon mutation; the inset shows a male of the Blue.

established in aviary stock are Lutino (yellow) and Blue forms, which have been effectively combined to produce the Albino, which shows no trace of colour pigment whatsoever.
Ring-necked Parakeets do not normally form a strong bond with their partner in the wild, and indeed, hens dominate their mates for most of the year. As a result, the psittaculid parakeets in general are not as satisfactory as pets compared with other psittacines. Yet they do become quite tame and will learn to speak a few words.

Ring-necks have a fairly defined breeding period, often nesting quite early in the year compared with other birds. The availability of young birds at certain times of the year can

therefore be a problem. The cock Ring-necked Parakeet will probably not acquire his characteristic collar until at least three years old, so that it is possible to age such birds with a degree of certainty. Kept under favourable conditions, Ring-necks can live for over half a century.

Related species, such as the Plumhead Parakeet (*Psittacula cyanocephala*), are too nervous to keep indoors unless they are housed in a small flight. Like the Ring-necked, their incubation period is about 23 days, and fledging usually occurs about seven weeks later.

Although many other attractive parakeets – notably from Australia – are widely bred in aviaries each year, these are not suitable for taming purposes. They tend to remain wild, even when obtained straight from the nest. It is the New World species that offer the greatest opportunity in this regard.

Lesser Sulphur-crested Cockatoo

Cacatua sulphurea
● **Distribution:** Sulawesi (Celebes) and adjoining islands.
● **Size:** 33cm (13in).
● **Diet:** Parrot mixture, plus fruit and greenstuff.
● **Immatures:** Clearly recognizable by their dark grey irises.

● **Sexing:** Mature hens are usually discernible by their reddish irises.
● **Pet appeal:** Lively and excitable.

Below:
Lesser Sulphur-crested Cockatoo
This cockatoo, the most widely kept as a pet bird, is prized for its intelligent and vivacious nature. Be sure to start with a young bird.

Moluccan Cockatoo
Cacatua moluccensis
● **Distribution:** South Moluccan islands, including Ceram and Amboina. (It appears to have been introduced into Amboina.)
● **Size:** 50cm (20in).
● **Diet:** Parrot mixture, plus fruit and greenstuff.
● **Immatures:** Can be distinguished by their grey irises.
● **Sexing:** Cocks invariably have black eyes; those of hens are brownish.
● **Pet appeal:** Large and spectacular.

The coloration of the Moluccan Cockatoo is very variable. Some of these birds are a deep shade of pink, whereas others are virtually white, like the closely related

Umbrella Cockatoo (*C. alba*). The pink feathering in the broad curved crest of all Moluccans distinguishes them, however, irrespective of the depth of their body plumage colour.

These cockatoos can be difficult to manage in view of their large size, destructive capabilities and harsh calls. Yet, if their conditions are favourable, young birds can become very tame and may display considerable affection towards their owners. Without adequate attention, however, these birds are liable to pluck their feathers and, once such behaviour has become established, it can be a very difficult problem to overcome (see page 19).

Right: **Moluccan Cockatoo**
A large cockatoo that needs care and attention; can become tame.

These unmistakable birds have long been popular as pets, but they can prove rather spiteful when in breeding condition. Before buying a cockatoo, always look closely at the plumage for any signs of the disease often described as feather rot (see pages 19-20). Brownish, twisted plumage may indicate this disc der in its early stages.

Cockatoos are confined essentially to Australasia, and this species has a discontinuous distribution over many islands. As a result, various distinctive subspecies are recognized, of which the best known is probably the Citron-crested (*C.s. citrinocristata*), from the island of Sumba. In this instance, the yellow crest and markings associated with the nominate race are replaced by orange feathering. There is also some variation in size between the different races; the smaller Timor subspecies (*C.s. parvula*), for example, does not exceed 25cm (10in) in overall size.

Left: **Citron-crested Cockatoo**
In this subspecies, the yellow crest and markings typical of the Lesser Sulphur Crested are distinctly orange in hue. Hand-reared cockatoos will become very tame.

Above: **Umbrella Cockatoo**
Generally less costly, but no less noisy than the related Moluccan.

Roseate Cockatoo
Eolophus roseicapillus
- **Distribution:** Over most of Australia.
- **Size:** 35.5cm (14in).
- **Diet:** Parrot mixture and cereal seeds, with fruit and greenstuff.
- **Immatures:** Grey irises and duller overall.
- **Sexing:** Cocks usually have darker irises than hens.
- **Pet appeal:** Colourful and quite docile.

These cockatoos are a pest species in parts of Australia, where they are often persecuted. Elsewhere, aviary strains do exist, but youngsters invariably command a high price. Roseates, which are also known as Galah Cockatoos, are quieter and

Above: **Roseate Cockatoos**
This photograph shows a normal form (left) alongside a mutation with white plumage and pink feet.

noticeably more docile than their predominantly white relatives. Their feeding requirements also appear to differ: avoid offering a diet based chiefly on sunflower and other oil seeds, since this can lead to the development of fatty tumours known as lipomas.

The depth of coloration can vary quite widely between individual birds, with some being significantly darker than others. A scarce mutation that results in the absence of melanin from the plumage causes the grey areas to be white and the feet to be pink.

Green-naped Lorikeet

Trichoglossus haematodus

- **Distribution:** Northern and eastern parts of Australia, and islands to the north and east.
- **Size:** 25cm (10in).
- **Diet:** Nectar and fruit, plus greenstuff and, possibly, some seed.
- **Immatures:** Dark, brownish beaks and brown irises.
- **Sexing:** No visual distinction possible between the sexes.
- **Pet appeal:** Lively, colourful and playful.

The lories and lorikeets include some of the most colourful members of the parrot family. There is no clearly defined means of distinguishing between lories and lorikeets, although it is usually accepted that lorikeets have longer tails than lories. Up to 21 races of the Green-naped Lorikeet are recognized; it is the island forms that are most commonly seen in avicultural circles outside Australia.

Although most are not easy to sex, pairs usually nest freely once established, and young birds are thus quite often available from breeders. Unfortunately, the major drawback of these lively parrots is their sticky, fluid droppings. It is best to site the cage on a cloth to protect the surroundings.

Below: **Green-naped Lorikeet**
These birds seem almost artificially coloured, so bright and precise are their markings. Active but messy.

Chattering Lory

Lorius garrulus

- **Distribution:** The Moluccan islands of Indonesia.
- **Size:** 30cm (12in).
- **Diet:** Nectar and fruit, with greenstuff and some seed.
- **Immatures:** Brown beaks and dark brown irises.
- **Sexing:** No visible means of distinguishing between the sexes.
- **Pet appeal:** Colourful and may even learn to talk.

These spectacular lories are often available, but unfortunately they are rather noisy. Again, their feeding habits make them somewhat unsuitable as pets, unless their accommodation can be cleaned very easily and thoroughly. In addition, they must have bathing facilities and they may splash water around the room.

Ensure that their diet is supplemented adequately with Vitamin A, since a deficiency can cause these birds to succumb to the fungal disease candidiasis. Also provide pollen, which is a natural food of this group of parrots. It is usually available from health food stores. Simply dissolve a few grains in the daily supply of nectar or sprinkle some on top of fruit.

Below: **Chattering Lory**
This flash photograph has caught this spectacular bird in mid chatter, ample proof of its garrulous nature!

Above: **Greater Hill Mynah**
An action shot of an incessantly lively bird. Aristocrats among mimics but need 'housekeeping'.

Greater Hill Mynah
Gracula religiosa
● **Distribution:** India, through Southeast Asia to Indonesia.
● **Size:** 30cm (12in).
● **Diet:** Softbill food or pellets, plus fruit and livefood, such as mealworms.
● **Immatures:** Duller, and lack wattles (fleshy skin flaps) on the head, which are characteristic of adults.
● **Sexing:** The sexes are similar, but cocks usually have more pronounced wattles.
● **Pet appeal:** Able mimics with lively natures.

Although various species are described as mynahs, it is the Greater Hill form and its subspecies, such as the large Javan race, which are the most highly valued as pets. Their powers of mimicry are vastly superior to those of related species.

Keeping a pet mynah bird is a time-consuming occupation, because of the time required to clean its quarters thoroughly. Newspaper on the floor of its accommodation will need changing at least once, and often twice daily. Perches must be washed off regularly, and the bird should be able to bath each day. A large earthenware dog bowl on the floor of the cage is ideal for this purpose, although you may want to screen the front of the cage with clear plastic sheeting during the bath to prevent surrounding carpets or furniture becoming soaked.

Mynahs are bold and active by nature, and will not prove shy like many parrots. Young birds are sometimes described as 'gapers', because they readily solicit hand-feeding by gaping with their beaks open. Towards the end of their lives, they may show signs of feather loss, with the lost feathers not being replaced. Ensure that these birds are kept in an even temperature, especially old individuals and particularly during the winter months, so that they do not develop chills and respiratory problems.

Domestic Canary

Serinus canarius domesticus

● **Distribution:** Does not occur in the wild.

● **Size:** Variable, from about 10cm (4in) to 20cm (8in) depending on the breed.

● **Diet:** Canary seed mixture, with plain canary seed and red rape, plus other seeds such as niger. Supply greenfood regularly.

● **Immatures:** Resemble adults but smaller, with shorter tails.

● **Sexing:** Cocks can be distinguished by their song.

● **Pet appeal:** Jaunty natures and cock birds have a lively song.

The early history of the Canary is unknown, but it seems clear that these finches are descended from the Wild Canaries (*S.c. canarius*), found on islands off the northwestern coast of Africa,

Below: **Lizard Canary**
An old and fascinating breed in which the plumage resembles a lizard's scales. Clear-capped form.

including the Canary Islands. Wild canaries were introduced to Europe, and may have been crossed with native songsters, such as the Serin (*S. serinus*). Early in the eighteenth century, yellow and white variants were recorded and selective breeding began in earnest, which has since given rise to the wide variety of breeds seen today.

The Lizard Canary, whose markings should resemble those of the reptile's scales, is one of the oldest breeds still in existence. The clear area of plumage often present on the head is described as a cap.

Some breeds have changed quite radically in appearance. The Yorkshire Canary, for example, named after the English county in which it was evolved, is now much broader than formerly. Canary breeds generally have remained localized, but some are well known internationally. Foremost among these is the Border Fancy, which was developed in the Border region between England and Scotland. This breed has attracted a strong

Above: **Yorkshire Canary**
Although broader than of old, this is still one of the slimmest breeds.

Below: **Clear Fife Canary**
The Fife reflects the original compactness of the Border Canary.

following among canary exhibitors, but is also popular with petseekers. Border Fancy canaries have been bred in a wide range of colours, but the yellow birds, described as 'Clears' are often the most popular. White canaries are also included in this 'Clear' category. Green birds and blues – really a shade of grey – are classed as selfs. Variegated colour forms are also common, as are cinnamons.

following among canary exhibitors, but is also popular with petseekers. Border Fancy canaries have been bred in a wide range of colours, but the yellow birds, described as 'Clears' are often the most popular. White canaries are also included in this 'Clear' category. Green birds and blues – really a shade of grey – are classed as selfs. Variegated colour forms are also common, as are cinnamons.

Recently, in a move to recapture the diminutive size of the original Border Fancy canaries, breeders have worked to create a smaller version, now recognized as the Fife Fancy. This breed is rapidly becoming very popular.

The crested mutation appears to have occurred quite early during the development of the canary fancy. Such birds were widely kept during the early years of the last century, but today, the smaller Gloster Fancy is the most popular member of the group. The breed itself only came to prominence after the Second World War, although its origins date back to the 1920s. The crested form in this instance is described as the Corona, whereas the non-crested form is known as the Consort. Coronas are not paired together, however, because of a lethal factor that affects the development of a proportion of the chicks and prevents them from hatching. If you

Above: **Gloster Corona Canary**
In this striking breed of canary, a crest forms a fringe over the eyes.

Below: **Gloster Consort Canaries**
The non-crested equivalents of the Gloster Corona. Be sure to use these when breeding cresteds.

want to breed these canaries, pairs should consist of one Corona and one Consort.

The other significant development during the present century has been the breeding of the New Coloured Canaries, of which the Red Factor is probably the best-

Above: **Red Factor Canary**
This elegant bird has so-called 'frosted' plumage, each soft-textured feather edged in white.

known example. Crossings involving a South American finch, the Hooded Siskin (*Carduelis cucullatus*), introduced orange-red coloration to the canary bloodline. Colour feeding at the time of the moult will ensure that the bird's colour is emphasized in the new plumage.

Singing canaries as pets
As we have seen, some canaries have been developed for their type (or physical appearance) and others for their coloration. A third group has been bred primarily for their singing ability and these are perhaps the most desirable as pets. The best-known example in this category is the Roller Canary, which originated in Germany, notably around the Harz Mountain region. Here, the birds were trained to mimic the sounds of mountain streams, emphasizing the purity of their song. Other breeds have been developed from Roller stock, of which the American Singer is probably the most widely known at present.

Various factors will influence your choice of pet canary. If you are interested in a songster, ensure that

Above: **Roller Canary**
*This classic breed of singing
canary – bred in Germany during
the 1600s – will make a tuneful pet.*

you obtain a cock, irrespective of
the colour or breed. Male canaries
usually sing quite readily, provided
they are not moulting. Housing two
birds in separate cages in the same
room often stimulates competition,
encouraging them both to sing for
long periods. Do not house two
cocks together, however, as they
are liable to fight.

While quality exhibition stock
often commands high price, birds of
less illustrious origins may be on
offer in pet stores. They will be quite
suitable as pets, provided you can
obtain a guarantee that the bird you
are considering is a cock. Before
you buy a canary, look closely at the
legs; if they are thickened and
heavily scaled, you can assume that
the bird is relatively old. Only if it has
a closed band on its leg will it be
possible to age the bird with
certainty. (A closed band is year
coded and often has the breeder's

club number and also a sequential
number to identify the chick. The
band is put on the chick's leg when it
is only a few days old.)

Breeding canaries in the home
You can breed canaries
successfully in the home,
accommodating them in a breeding
cage with a nesting pan attached
inside. The pan should be lined with
a piece of felt, and the hen provided
with special safe nesting material
available from your pet store. The
hen canary usually lays a total of
four eggs, producing one egg each
day. It is common practice to
remove the first three eggs, store
them in a matchbox lined with
cotton wool and replace them with
dummy eggs. On the fourth day –
when the final egg is expected –
restore the real eggs to the hen and
she will start to incubate them. This
technique ensures that the chicks
will be of similar age when they
hatch, and thus more likely to
survive. It is usual to remove the
cock bird just before egg laying, and
to allow the hen to rear the chicks on

her own. Alternatively, the pair can be left together throughout.

The incubation period is about 13 days. The young canaries leave the nestpan after a similar period of time, and are independent within a further week or so. Offer a special rearing food throughout this period and introduce hard seed gradually.

Above: *A hen canary incubating the eggs in a nestpan, suitably lined with a piece of felt. Four eggs make up the usual clutch.*

Below: *A canary with a closed band on its leg. The band is stamped with details that will enable you to determine its age.*

Zebra Finch

Poephila guttata

● **Distribution:** Over much of Australia, except the Cape York Peninsula, and certain southern areas. Also occurs on the Flores Islands, to the northwest of Australia.
● **Size:** 10cm (4in).
● **Diet:** Mixed millets, plain canary seed and greenfood.
● **Immatures:** Dark beaks.
● **Sexing:** Hens have paler beaks, and lack the markings on the breast and flanks of the cock.
● **Pet appeal:** Adaptable and easy to breed. Vivacious nature.

Zebra Finches have been domesticated for many years and numerous colour varieties are now well established. The White mutation is one of the earliest recorded, dating back to 1921. Here, birds of both sexes are pure white in colour. A separate, yet similar, mutation is the Chestnut-

Right: **Chestnut-flanked White**
This is a cock bird, as shown by the spotted markings on the flanks. One of many colour forms.

Below: **Fawn Zebra Finch**
Here, the male retains its distinctive markings but the colour is an overall pale shade of brown.

flanked White. In this instance, cock birds retain their typical markings offset against a white body coloration. The Fawn Zebra Finch – a warm shade of brown – is another of the more common varieties.

In Zebra Finches, as with the Budgerigar, a mutation has occurred which modifies, or dilutes the colour, but is not a colour in its own right. When combined with the normal Grey form, the result is described as the Silver; in conjunction with the Fawn, a Cream is produced.

The Pied mutation of the Zebra Finch can show any of these colours offset against white, with a highly variable distribution of markings. While other mutations, such as the

Yellow-beaked, remain scarce, the Crested is becoming more widespread. The crest in this instance forms a full circle on the head. As with similar mutations in other species, these birds are not paired together, but with non-crested stock. Like the Pied, the crested mutation can be combined with any colour.

Zebra Finches will breed quite regularly in the home if they are provided with a breeding cage and small nestbox, or even just a finch nesting basket. However, once the nest is complete and the hen has laid, be sure to withhold further supplies of nesting material. Otherwise, the birds may continue building, obscuring their eggs in the process. Under normal circumstances, up to six eggs will be laid. These hatch after 12 days or so, and both birds share the task of incubation. Rearing food, supplied fresh each day, and removed on the same evening before it sours, will help to ensure that the chicks are reared satisfactorily. They fledge at about 18 days old, and will feed independently within a fortnight.

At this stage the adults are likely to be nesting again, so now is the time to remove the young birds. Restrict hens to rearing no more than three rounds of chicks in succession, by removing the nesting facilities. Overbreeding is liable to lead to eggbinding. An eggbound hen is unable to lay the egg, and it creates an obstruction in her body. In small birds especially, this condition may prove fatal. Under normal circumstances, however, Zebra Finches are very easy birds to keep and breed successfully in the home.

·Left: **White Zebra Finch**
One of the original mutations seen in Zebra Finches. There are no visible differences between sexes.

Below: **Cream Zebra Finch**
The diluting effect of this mutation has toned down the colours of the Fawn into pale creams. A male.

Above: **Self Chocolate Bengalese**
This is one of the standard colour forms of these lively finches. Celebrated throughout the world for their friendly nature and willingness to breed, Bengalese are ideal for beginners to finches.

Above right: **Self Fawn Bengalese**
Self or single-coloured Bengalese are less common than pied forms.

Below: **Fawn & White Bengalese**
These birds show the wide colour variation possible in pied forms.

Bengalese Finch

Lonchura striata domestica
● **Distribution:** Does not occur in the wild.
● **Size:** 10cm (4in).
● **Diet:** Millets and other small cereal seeds, plus greenstuff.

● **Immatures:** Duller and paler.
● **Sexing:** No visual means of distinguishing the sexes, but cock birds may be recognized by their song when in breeding condition.
● **Pet appeal:** Compatible and breeds readily.

Like the previous species, the Bengalese Finch can be kept and bred quite satisfactorily in groups, provided that sufficient nesting sites are available. The origins of these members of the Munia group are unclear; their ancestry probably derives from the Sharp-tailed Munia (*L. striata*) and they may have been first domesticated in China.

Bengalese, better known in the United States as Society Finches, have been bred in a range of colours. Dark brown birds are described as Self Chocolate, and their lighter counterparts are known as Self Fawns. Pied variants, such as the Fawn and White, are equally common, while a Chestnut variant is becoming increasingly popular, both in self and pied forms. The Self White, which is pure in colour like all Selfs, is scarce, although it was the first example of the Bengalese seen in Europe, in 1860. A crested mutation has also occurred.

The breeding habits of the Bengalese are similar to those of Zebra Finches, although the clutch size is often larger. The chicks may not fledge until they are more than three weeks old and are mature by nine months of age.

113

Index to species

Page numbers in **bold** indicate major references, including accompanying photographs. Page numbers in *italics* indicate captions to other illustrations. Less important text entries are shown in normal type.

Further reading

Alderton, D. *Looking after Cage Birds* Ward Lock, 1982
Alderton, D. *Beginner's Guide to Lovebirds* Paradise Press, 1984
Alderton, D. *Beginner's Guide to Zebra Finches* Paradise Press, 1984
Alderton, D. *The Complete Cage and Aviary Bird Handbook* Pelham Books, 1986
Arnall, L. & Keymer, I.F. *Bird Diseases* Balliere Tindall, 1975
Bracegirdle, J. *The Border Canary* Saiga Publishing, 1981
Cross, J.S. *The Gloster Fancy Canary* Saiga Publishing, 1978
Dodwell, G.T. *Encyclopedia of Canaries* TFH Publications, 1976
Dodwell, G.T. *The Lizard Canary and Other Rare Breeds* Triplegate, 1982
Forshaw, J.M. *Parrots of the World* David and Charles, 1978
Harper, D. *Pet Birds for Home and Garden* Salamander Books, 1986
Howson, E. *The Yorkshire Canary* Saiga Publishing, 1980
Immelmann, K. *Australian Finches* Angus and Robertson, 1982
Jennings, G. *Beginner's Guide to Parrots* Paradise Press, 1985
Low, R. *Mynah Birds* Bartholomew, 1976
Low, R. *Parrots – Their Care and Breeding* Blandford Press, 1986
Martin, R.M. *Cage and Aviary Birds* Collins, 1980
Rutgers, A. & Novis, K.A. (Editors) *Encyclopedia of Aviculture* (Volumes II and III) Blandford Press, 1977
Smith, G.A. *Encyclopedia of Cockatiels* TFH Publications, 1978
Vince, C. *Keeping Softbilled Birds* Stanley Paul, 1980
Walker, G.B.R. *Coloured Canaries* Blandford Press, 1976
Watmough, W. & Rogers, C.H. *The Cult of the Budgerigar* Nimrod Book Services, 1984

Picture credits

Artists
Copyright of the artwork illustrations on the pages following the artists' names is the property of Salamander Books Ltd.

Alan Harris: 14, 22, 39, 47, 55, 63

Seb Quigley (Linden Artists): 16

Photographs
Unless otherwise stated, all the photographs have been taken by and are the copyright of Cyril Laubscher.
The publishers wish to thank the following photographers who have supplied other photographs for this book. The photographs have been credited by page number and position on the page: (B)Bottom, (T)Top, (C)Centre, (BL)Bottom left etc.

Ideas into Print: 18, 55(T), 68(TR)

Martin Lawton: 56(TL,TR,BL), 58(BL,BR), 59(T,B)

Tessa Musgrave © Salamander Books: 34-5, 36, 40-1, 42-3, 52

John Stoodley: 85

Acknowledgements
The publishers wish to thank the following for their help in preparing this book: Chris Allaway; Ghalib-Al-Nasser; Paul and June Bailey; Eric Barlow; Blean Bird Park; Irene Christie; Mick and Marion Cripps; Karen Docherty; Jackie Donaghy; Alan Donnelly; Ken and Shirley Epps; Ray and Kathleen Fisk; Kevin Fraser; Simon Gage; Rodney and Joan Hamilton; John and Adrianne Holland; Sarah Kelly; Tim Kemp; Debra Kenyon; George Lewsey; Gary McCarthy; Stanley Maughan; Albert and Monica Newsham; Oaklands Park Farm Aviaries; Ron Oxley; John Plommer; Mick and Beryl Plose; Gordon Plumb; Porter's Cage Bird Appliances; Harold Prater; Ron Rayner; Sue Sikora; Stan and Jill Sindel; Charlie and Jane Smith; Brian Spendley; Steve Stephenson; Nigel Taboney; Alan Tinham; Whites Pet Centre; Cliff Wright. Rita Hemsley (for typing the author's manuscript); Amanda Harrison and Karen Ramsay (for editorial assistance.)

Red Factor Canary